The Life Of Admiral Sir Isaac Coffin, Baronet, His English And American Ancestors;

Amory, Thomas C. (Thomas Coffin), 1812-1889. cn

Nabu Public Domain Reprints:

You are holding a reproduction of an original work published before 1923 that is in the public domain in the United States of America, and possibly other countries. You may freely copy and distribute this work as no entity (individual or corporate) has a copyright on the body of the work. This book may contain prior copyright references, and library stamps (as most of these works were scanned from library copies). These have been scanned and retained as part of the historical artifact.

This book may have occasional imperfections such as missing or blurred pages, poor pictures, errant marks, etc. that were either part of the original artifact, or were introduced by the scanning process. We believe this work is culturally important, and despite the imperfections, have elected to bring it back into print as part of our continuing commitment to the preservation of printed works worldwide. We appreciate your understanding of the imperfections in the preservation process, and hope you enjoy this valuable book.

ADMIRAL SIR ISAAC COFFIN.

His Britannic Majesty's Ship Alligator
Boston Harbor 5th May 1791

Isaac Coffin

THE LIFE

OF

ADMIRAL

SIR ISAAC COFFIN,

BARONET

HIS ENGLISH AND AMERICAN ANCESTORS

BY

THOMAS C. AMORY

BOSTON
CUPPLES, UPHAM AND COMPANY
1886

Copyright 1886, by
THOMAS C. AMORY

TROW'S
PRINTING AND BOOKBINDING COMPANY,
NEW YORK.

PREFACE.

THIS memoir, in its original form of a discourse, had its limitations of time and topic. Much else might have been added connected with the subject had the occasion allowed. The several histories of Nantucket, the "Life of Tristram Coffin," by Mr Allen Coffin, of "General John Coffin," by his son, Henry Edward; "The Arms of the Family," by Mr. John Coffin Jones Brown, are well known and accessible. Other sources of information exist in print and manuscript. Bearing in mind that many readers of these pages will find them more instructive if they have at hand what will better explain them, I have borrowed from their pages, under marks of quotation, in the larger part by permission and with grateful acknowledgments. If I have been too bold, I pray their forgiveness. Let me also express my sense of the kindness of the New York Genealogical and Biographical Society, in permitting me to read what portions of this memoir their limits permitted, in their course. and to have these portions, somewhat extended, inserted in their January *Record.*

BOSTON, *March* 1, 1886.

CONTENTS.

		PAGE
I —Ancestry		7
II —Alwington		13
III —New England		18
IV. —Nantucket		21
V —Tristram's Death and Descendants		25
VI. —Boston and Isaac Coffin		31
VII —Isaac at Sea		36
VIII —Captain of a Seventy-four		41
IX —Peace of 1783		44
X. —Marriage and Parliament		48
XI —Genial Temperament		51
XII —Benefactions and Death		54
XIII —The Coffin Coats of Arms		60
XIV —Tuckett's Visitations of Devon		63
XV —Coffin Dates		64
XVI —The Reformation		66
XVII —Allen Coffin's Call of Tristram's Descendants to the Second Centennial of his Death in 1881		68
XVIII—Wills		78
XIX —Correspondence		85
XX. —The Coffin Schools		96

THE LIFE OF
ADMIRAL SIR ISAAC COFFIN, BART.

I.

ANCESTRY.

THE name of Coffin is so widely spread over our continent, so many thousands of men and women of other patronymics take pride in their descent from Tristram, its first American patriarch, that what concerns them all, any considerable branch or distinguished individual of the race, seems rather history than biography.

Space forbids my repeating here, as I well might wish, all that has been recorded of their existence in the new world, or that beyond the sea. But what sheds light on Sir Isaac and his immediate progenitors is too germane to my subject to be wholly overlooked. To trace back Tristram to Alwington, follow his fortunes from Plympton in old England to the Merrimack in the new, bring his checkered career to its honored close at Nantucket; to pay due homage to his son James, the upright judge; to his son Nathaniel, the dauntless master mariner, and his wife, Damaris Gayer, the eloquent preacher; to their son William, the much-loved merchant of Boston, senior warden of Trinity; to his son, another Nathaniel, graduate of Harvard and Yale, King's treasurer, and father of Sir Isaac—six generations with Tristram of admirable men, with much to praise and little to censure, is our legitimate purpose, so far as our limits prescribed will permit, before proceeding to our more immediate subject.

Though unlike in character, and of very different experiences from his ancestors, Sir Isaac was too remarkable a man to pass into oblivion. His long life, commencing in 1759 in Boston, and ending eighty years later in Cheltenham, England, was crowded with events, many of historic importance. By his native vigor, doughty deeds, and eminent services he rose to distinguished rank in the British navy, became captain of a line-of-battle ship at the age of twenty-two, and was created a baronet at the age of forty-four. This not from large means, family influence, or court favor, but that his character and conduct afloat and ashore entitled him to such preferment. Throngs of heroic officers won glory in the same wars that he did, attracted attention by more conspicuous achievements; but his fearless daring, zeal, and ability, and what he accomplished, inscribes his memory high up on the roll of honor, if not on the scroll of fame.

How far life and character are moulded by circumstances, how far by heredity, is a complicated problem, and the horoscope is too largely affected by maternal influences for these to be disregarded. Though bearing all the marks of his paternal stock, Sir Isaac doubtless owed something to the blood mingling in his veins from other sources, and it has been my endeavor to discover these infusions where I can, and one instance should be preserved for the criticism of coming genealogists—a supposed link that may be of use.

Nicholas, father of Peter and grandfather of Tristram, has been regarded as their most remote paternal ancestor ascertained. According to tradition, their line was an offshoot of Alwington, but how, continued a puzzle. Many years ago I bought an old edition of Collins (1758), and while seeking some other information, my eyes fell on the name of Peter Coffin, who about 1560 married Mary, fourth daughter of Hugh Boscawen. Hugh died 1559, at the age of eighty. As the homes of the Boscawens, Tregothnan and Penkeville, lay near Brixton, the home of Tristram, this awakened curiosity, the more that Peter's name was not in the index, and might have escaped the notice of previous genealogical inquirers.

Hugh Boscawen, of one of the most affluent and influential families of Cornwall, married Phillippa Carminow, of large possessions and royal descent, inheriting, through Philip Courtenay, the unfortunate Marquis of Exeter, Plympton, and other estates near Plymouth, part of which we find the inheritance of Tristram. Hugh had seven sons and seven daughters. The third son, Nicholas, eighty-six when he died in 1626, was the successor of his parents in their estates. His sister Mary, who married Peter Coffin, must have been born about 1545, as there were nine younger children than herself born before 1559, when her father died at the age of eighty. Her brass at Penkeville gives her death in 1622. Her age is not very clearly stated, but apparently as seventy-seven. Her son Nicholas, if grandfather of Tristram, would have been of an age, in 1582, to have been father of Peter, who died 1628, and whose wife Joanna, mother of Tristram, died in Boston, 1661, aged seventy-seven, having been born in 1584.

If thus, or in any other way, connected with the Coffins, the house of Tregothnan is too historical, and associated with too many important events in our colonial annals, not to make it worthy of note. Lord Falmouth, under Queen Anne, Edward, the commander of the British fleet in the second reduction of Louisbourg, in more recent days, have added to the lustre of a name prolific in naval heroes and eminent statesmen. The importance we attach to this supposed connection is that it affords clews to ascertain the relation of Tristram to Alwington, and as Petronel, the sister of Mrs. Peter Coffin, married Peter Mayhowe, a possible explanation how Thomas Mayhew and Tristram Coffin here together planted Nantucket. Tuckett's Devon Visitations, full as to the main male line of Alwington, are being carried back, extended out, and brought down by Colonel Vivyan, who is approaching the Coffins. My suggestions may help his researches, and they are given for what they are worth.

But who was the father of Peter Coffin, who married Mary Boscawen? He must have been born about 1500. If among the recorded members of the family are found individuals whose dates or other known circumstances are inconsistent with the parentage of Peter, that reduces the field of investigation. Sceptical minds reject hypothesis in such researches, but often hypothesis, fairly tested, is the only path to the truth. At Monkley, about ten miles east from Portlege, one of the homes of its junior branches, dwelt at the time James, son of Richard and Miss Chudleigh, whose brother John married Mary Cary. His wife, Mary Cole, was the near kinswoman of William, who married Radigan, daughter of Nicholas Boscawen. Tristram named his sons after his ancestors. James was his fourth son. These circumstances amount to nothing as proof, but may lead to it, or perhaps confirm the conclusion of Mr. Allen Coffin, that the connection with Alwington, if any, is much more remote. Near the close will be found an article on this and other kindred topics, portions of which by his permission I insert.

In the sequel will be found the visitation of the Coffins of Portlege. Its examination will show other grounds on which we rest our faith as to the parentage of Peter. It will be seen that in the sixth generation John Coffin married Philippa, daughter and co-heiress of Phillip Hingston. His eldest son Richard, Sheriff of Devon in 1511 (2 Hen. VIII), married Wilmot, daughter of Sir Richard Chudleigh, famous in legal annals as party in a leading case which bears his name. This marriage took place about 1510. The Sheriff had three sons, John, James, and Edward. The second, James, born as late as 1512, might well have been father of Peter, who, about 1562, married Mary Boscawen. Their son Nicholas, if born in 1563, would have been old enough in 1585 to have been father of Peter, who, the father of Tristram, died in 1628 Wedlock came early when there were few other distractions. Under favorable circumstances life was often prolonged beyond the average limit, but war, exposure, perhaps inferior medical skill, backwardness of medical science, sufficiently explain why so many failed to live out their allotted span. As the line consists mainly of eldest sons, less time embraced these several generations

The best known of the brothers of the Sheriff, Sir William, born about 1480, going to Court, stood high in the estimation of Henry the Eighth Like Raleigh, later from the same province, he won his way by his wit and courage. He was selected in 1519 by the King as one of the eighteen English knights to take part in the tournament before Guines, in France, with a like number of French gentlemen, practised in arms and renowned for prowess He was Master of Horse at the coronation of Anne Boleyn, and appointed one of the gentlemen of the King's Privy Chamber, filled to the monarch's satisfaction a position of distinction and influence much coveted at Court. He married Margaret, the daughter of Sir George Dimock, the champion of England, and from her, after his death the wife of Richard Manners, descended the later Dukes of Rutland. Sir William took a prominent part in the Parliament, one ecclesiastical abuse being done away with at his instance.* At Standon, a royal manor, of which he was high steward when he died in 1538, stands his monument He left no children, and by his will devised his lands to his brother Richard's sons, bequeathed his hawks, hounds, and hunting gear to the King His brothers James and Thomas had children, but the dates confirm the view that his nephew, James, and Mary Cole were the parents of Peter, who married Mary Boscawen.

Doubtless there were other branches of the name, from among which we might look for the ancestry of Tristram His earliest progenitors in England came over with the Conqueror in 1066. Captain Henry Coffin, in his memoir of General John Coffin, 1880, says that several years before he had visited Falaise, in Normandy, and near that place lay estates owned eight centuries earlier by the Coffins, before they crossed over the Channel to the land of promise. These estates were still the property of their descendants in the female line Falaise will be remembered as the birthplace of the Conqueror. It is said that the name of Coffin was a corruption or translation of Colvinus, signifying a basket or chest, and that from

---

* This act, limiting the amount of mortuaries, the fees of the parish priest for burial, has been counted one of three statutes mentioned by the historians as ecclesiastical reforms which, from the abuses done away and the debates they provoked, helped to bring about the Reformation

charge of the King's treasure—such employment, like royalty itself, being hereditary—the name attached to the family. The confidence implied by its responsible duties seems explained by the integrity which has been characteristic of all their successive generations. Such virtue was its own reward, and if too generous to be noted for many instances of affluence, they even in that regard were prospered as they multiplied and spread over the earth.

Of the first who came over to England little seems known. Westcote tells us that Alwington in 1085, according to Domesday, was possessed by David De la Bere, and that the heiress of that name brought it to the Coffins. On a subject less grave this might be suspected for a jest, but the authority is proof. Sir William Pole, page 386, states that Sir Richard Coffin held two knights' fees there from Robert, the King's son, in the reign of Henry II. Whether earlier than this or later, flourished branches of that name at Combe Coffin, now Combe Pine, in the east of Devon, at Coffin Well, in the south, and at Ingarley in the west, Sir Hugh, Sir Elias, Sir Geoffry, are mentioned in the records later than the first of a long line of Richards who, with some breaks in the continuity of name and knighthood, held Alwington and dwelt there. At Coffin's Ingarley once stood a noble mansion, with a church near by, surrounded by an extensive deer park. Its lord, Sir Elias, about 1200, bore gilded spurs in token of his military rank, and Sir Hugh, of Combe Coffin, his contemporary, was similarly distinguished. They may have been offshoots of Alwington, or that branch of theirs. From among them might possibly have proceeded our branch in this country, but we think not.

It must not be forgotten that in the pedigree of Coffin in "the Devon Visitations" there is mention made of a Nicholas, who, so far as regards dates, could not have been Tristram's grandfather. Richard, the sheriff, 1511, was born in all probability thirty years at the least before he was made sheriff. His son John, born about 1510, married Mary Cary, and their second son, John, born after 1569, was not of an age before 1589 to be married. His wife was Grace Berry, daughter of Richard of Berrynarbor. Their third son, Nicholas, aged seven when the visitation was made, probably in 1620, must have been born in 1613, in which year Nicholas, father of Peter, who died in 1628, and grandfather of our Tristram, passed away.

It is well also to bear in mind, in connection with this inquiry as to the ancestry of Tristram, that Anna, daughter of Sir William Chudleigh, who died in 1515, married James Coffin, of Portlege, brother of the Sheriff. Her niece Wilmot, daughter of Sir Richard Chudleigh, who died

1558, was the wife of the Sheriff. As the eldest son of Sir Richard Chudleigh, Christopher, was thirty years and more at his father's death, Wilmot might seem to have been much younger than her husband. Still, the expression, "thirty years and more," in legal documents, at the period, was very indefinite It seemed to leave open the question whether James Coffin and Anna Chudleigh are among the possibilities for the parentage of Peter, great-grandfather of Tristram, James, the Sheriff's son, and Mary Cole, or others yet to be discovered.

II.

ALWINGTON.

But why seek to trace Tristram's lineage to Alwington? The beauty of the place, the character of its long line of proprietors through seven hundred years—one of the very few instances, even in England, in which an estate has remained for so great a length of time in the same family—which has never been sold, sequestered, or confiscated, or passed except by inheritance, will, or family settlement, which has continued not only their chief but constant habitation, suggests a home so enduring, qualities so sterling, that in a world changeable as this it is solacing to every conservative element in our nature to believe we too belong to it

Alwington extends along the Severn Sea, south of the boundary between Somerset and Devon, fronting the broad Atlantic. The mighty billows roll in majestic force against its cliffs and crags. The domain now embraces thirty-eight * hundred acres, part in fertile farms with substantial steadings; part in park and pleasure-grounds, studded with forest trees in clumps and woods. Its area may have expanded in prosperous days, or been shorn down to provide for junior branches, but its grounds are substantially the same now as under the Plantagenets, or when it first came to the Coffins with the heiress of the De la Beres.

When we call to mind what this beautiful region embraces from the Severn Sea to its southern shores, Exmoor and Dartmoor, which Blackmore and Kingsley have so brilliantly described, its romantic streams and majestic hills, with their wild sublimity—and who has not read "Lorna Doon"—we can well consider it a privilege that such associations cluster about our own ancestral memories, that the Coffins and so many Americans from Devon have such good reason to be proud of their mother-country, feel deeper interest in their progenitors that they dwelt amid scenes so picturesque. Our kinswoman, Mrs. Johnson, will pardon me if I draw in part from her own eloquent account of Portlege what will convey a more perfect idea of the place.

The approach from Bideford in Somersetshire south to Portlege, the manor-house of Alwington, extends for four miles along a shaded road, lined

---

* Late census.

on either side with luxuriant hedges, brambled vines, and grasses. Half a mile from the house the road reaches the great gateway, which opens on grounds tastefully disposed ; for time and taste and means effect marvels about the old homes of England. Lawns and gardens in a fine state of cultivation spread around, with that depth of verdure and coloring peculiar to the proximity to the sea, for in Devon the grape and peach, if protected, ripen beside the pear and plum

The house sets low for shelter from the blasts, and is not conspicuous until closely approached. The spirit of repose that it breathes, of the times that have passed, of the various vicissitudes of sorrow and enjoyment that have cheered or tried its generations, noted for their culture and refinement as they have come and passed from infancy to age, cannot escape your attention in the photograph of the edifice.

About the same distance from the house. along the shore, stretches a beach looking out over the Atlantic, to which a shaded walk from the house winds among ferns and groves thick with shrubs and rich with various verdure. Seats judiciously disposed afford a resting-place for the enjoyment of the view and the breeze. About a mile away stands the old church, bosked in mossy foliage, quiet and secluded, no dwelling in sight, venerable with age, if too substantial for decay. Its pews of oak, black with time, are richly carved, as often seen in these ancient shrines Here more than twenty generations have brought their children in arms to the font, their dead for sepulchre. Here their blooming maidens, their own or their tenants', have come to be joined in wedlock. The walls and floors of the edifice, as the burial ground around it, are crowded with slabs and monuments that relate, with the same touching simplicity, the annals of them all.

Within the walls of the mansion, which are of stone, with coigns and buttresses and battlements, windows varied but harmonious, is a large, square entrance hall with gallery on the level of the second floor. This and the spacious dining-room are lined with family portraits, men and women in antiquated garb, representing the blue eyes and characteristic features of the race Carved doors abound of stately dimensions, and ceilings of faded grandeur, displaying in many colors the emblazonments and quarterings of the family arms and of others of the best, connected with them by marriage. Many are derived from royal and noble progenitors— Pomeroys, Beaumonts, Chudleighs, Courtenays, Prideaux, Carys, Champernouns, Cliffords, Bassets, Damerels, of Devon or adjacent counties. Imagination conjures up the throng of these personages, long mouldered, as on festal occasions they gathered to the banquet or the dance, roamed and wooed by the moonbeams, shot arrows at the targe, let loose the falcon, or rode after the hounds.

The ancient forms and arrangements of the mansion, modified to meet as well the requirements of modern taste and comfort as to retain what is old or quaint, combine to constitute Portlege a most agreeable home to dwell in. It was once famous for its precious and extensive library, its archives rich with the accumulations of many generations. Sad to say, about 1800, in the transfer under a settlement to another branch, the books were mostly sold and many documents dispersed. There still remain vast coffers of manuscript treasures, which in time must perish, but which should, before too late, be arranged, copied, translated into intelligible language, calendared, catalogued, and indexed. Some antiquary of the family may yet be born to the faith that he can devote his days to no better field of service to posterity than such a task.

Before taking leave of Alwington, as Tristram's progenitors passed off from the ancestral stem, an enumeration of the succeeding generations from John and Mary Cary may be of interest. Their second son wedded Grace, daughter of Richard Berrie, of Berrianarbor; Richard, the oldest, 1569-1617 (forty-eight), Elizabeth, 1571-1651 (aged eighty), daughter of Leonard Lovels, of Cornwall. With the eight sons and seven daughters of Richard, as they grew into life, Portlege must have been gay, and as the daughters, at least, followed in rapid succession to their nuptials, not even what was disagreeable in the Stuart monarchs or the contentions of the land could have cast a shadow so remote from the court and battle-field. When the mother died, in 1651, James, the fifth son and last survivor, erected in the church of Alwington a monument to the memory of his parents, with an inscription which tells in rude rhymes their story. The eldest of the two sons left two daughters, Jane and Elizabeth, and the inheritance passed to a second Richard, 1622-99, "Without an enemy while living, and universally lamented when dead." His wife was Ann Prideaux, daughter of Edmund, of Padstow, 1645-1705, who died at the age of sixty. He was much esteemed, and in 1686 was sheriff of Devon under James II.

The children of the sheriff and Ann Prideaux were Bridget, John, Honora, and Richard. The eldest son married Ann Kellond, travelled extensively over Europe, stood well for character and scholarship, but died at the age of twenty-five in 1703. Honora married Richard Bennett; Dorothy, Richard Pyne, from whom came the Pyne Coffins. Richard, who succeeded his brother John in 1703, for seventy-three years was lord of Alwington, and died there in 1776 unmarried. He settled the estates first on the Bennetts, Robert and Richard, who died without children; and the reversion went to the Pynes descended from Honora, who took the name of Coffin. The present proprietor, born 1841, was the grandson of Richard, great-grandson of the youngest daughter of the sheriff, who died 1699, and Ann Prideaux, who died 1705. As Mr. Pyne Coffin has a large family of fine healthy children, there seems no chance of any of the male line of the Coffins ever succeeding to Alwington.

It is believed the male representation of the family rests in some descendant of Peter Coffin, who about 1560 married Mary Boscawen. A few words remain to be said about them. Phillippa Carminow, mother of Mrs. Mary Coffin, was, as already mentioned, co-heiress of that part of the Courtenay estates which escaped forfeiture when the Marquis of Exeter, next to the crown, was beheaded. Plympton, near the home of Tristram, formed part of the Courtenay inheritance which Phillippa Carminow carried to Hugh Boscawen, of Tregothnan, 1469-1559, as his wife. Their home was at Penkevil, not far up the river from Brixton, and is still the home of the Lords of Falmouth, their representatives. Evidence is found in an inquisition of William and Mary, 1558, of the Coffins, of Portlege, holding lands at Plympton, which may have come through the Boscawen's by this marriage, or perhaps may have led to it. At Plympton and Brixton Nicholas, grandfather of Tristram, and Peter, his father, resided; and Tristram took, by the will of his father, Peter, subject to his mother's life estate, these lands, or a part of them, which it would seem likely came in this way or through the Hingstons.

Many have searched for the ancestral line of Tristram among the records of Devonshire. No one has as yet been able, as already stated, to trace with certainty his pedigree beyond that of his grandfather, Nicholas Coffyn. Sir Isaac, in memorializing the College of Arms, in 1804, for the grant of a coat for himself, represented that he was by tradition descended from the family of Coffin, of the west of England, but that he was unable to ascertain his descent. No doubt seems entertained, however, that the proper investigation of the matter will some time reveal Tristram's true pedigree extending much further back; if not that suggested, what is now unknown will prove as honorable as that which we now know with reasonable certainty.

Tristram Coffyn, of Butler's Parish, of Brixton, County of Devon, England, made his will November 16, 1601, which was proved at Totness, in the same county, in 1602.

He left legacies to Joan, Anne, and John, children of Nicholas Coffyn; Richard and Joan, children of Lionel Coffyn; Philip Coffyn, and his son Tristram; and appointed Nicholas, son of Nicholas Coffyn, his executor. He was probably the great-uncle of the first of the race in America.

Nicholas Coffyn, of Brixton (one account says Butler's Parish), in Devonshire, in his will, dated September 12, 1613, and proved November 3, 1613, mentions his wife Joan, and sons Peter, Nicholas, Tristram, John, and daughter Anne He was the grandfather of the emigrant to New England, and born about 1560, probably the son of Mary Boscawen He lived to the end of the reign of the Tudors, and saw the reign of the Stuarts commenced in the person of James VI of Scotland and I. of England. He died in the reign of James I. (1613) His eldest son, Peter, doubtless succeeded to his estates, and his youngest son, John, acquired some estate, as he made our Tristram his executor. The other sons, Nicholas and Tristram, have not been accounted for, neither has his daughter Anne

Peter Coffyn, of Brixton, in his will, dated December 1, 1627, and proved March 13, 1628, provides that his wife Joan (Thember) shall have possession of the land during her life, and then the said property shall go to his son and heir, Tristram, "who is to be provided for according to his degree and calling." His son John is to have certain property when he becomes twenty years of age He mentions his daughters Joan, Deborah, Eunice, and Mary, and refers to his tenement in Butler's Parish, called Silferhay. He was the father of the emigrant.

John Coffyn, of Brixton, an uncle of the emigrant, who died without issue, in his will, dated January 4, 1628, and proved April 3, 1628, appoints his nephew, Tristram Coffyn, his executor, and gives legacies to all of Tristram's sisters, all under twelve years of age.

III.

NEW ENGLAND.

WHAT motives induced Tristram, in 1642, to dispose of so pleasant an abode and come to America can be conjectured, but are not positively known It has been said that he had been employed as colonel in command of the garrison at Plymouth, but this is not authenticated, and may have referred to his uncle Tristram; but we do know that in its defence his only brother, John, had been slain. Tristram had married, at the early period customary in those primitive times, Dionis Stevens, and had already five children—Peter, Tristram, Elizabeth, James, and John

As his brother John was killed at Plymouth Fort, it may be that Tristram was in the fight. The Stuarts made sorry kings, and the resistance they provoked to their arbitrary rule seems justified But England was seething on the verge of twenty years of contention, and Tristram, not over-fond of either party, and imperilled by the part he had taken, with ten women and children in his charge, may have been glad to escape persecution for them and himself in America. Two of his four sisters married in Devon. Two, Mary and Eunice, with their mother, his wife, and five children, accompanied him in 1642, the year King Charles placed himself in open array against the parliament.

That he came in that of the four vessels—Hector, Griffin, Job Clement, and Margaret Clement, belonging to Captain Robert Clement, that came over in 1642, which Captain Clement himself commanded—is well authenticated. It is known that after a brief residence at Salisbury, he moved up the river that year to what is now the next town, Haverhill, to form that settlement with Clement, on land bought from the Sachem Pasconaway.

With this large and dependent family of nine women and children, Tristram crossed the sea, disembarking at the mouth of the Merrimac, where they so long made their home The births of his other children born in America show the different periods he resided in Salisbury, Haverhill, on the north of the river, and at Newbury, to its south. We have no knowledge of his going far from that neighborhood during the next sixteen years, till he went to Nantucket, though it seems reasonable to suppose that he did so.

The property they brought sufficed to support in comfort the families of his mother and his own, and to establish respectably in marriage, as they grew up, his sisters and his sons. He first settled himself at Salisbury, in the three-mile space between the Merrimack and the New Hampshire border, as fixed by the patent; but removed that year to Haverhill, adjoining Salisbury, up the river, for in 1642, in November, his name is attached to an Indian deed there. There Mary, afterward Mrs. Starbuck, was born, and John the first having died, another took his place. In 1648 Tristram removed to Newbury, where his youngest son, Stephen, was added to the family group. After residing there for several years, during which he was licensed to keep an inn and a ferry over the Merrimack, Tristram returned to Salisbury, where he became a county magistrate.

Salisbury was close to the border of New Hampshire, and his eldest son, Peter, a merchant and king's counsellor in Dover, in that province, not far removed from Salisbury, married, about 1657, Abigail, daughter of Edward Starbuck; and his second son, Tristram, in 1653, Judith, daughter of Captain Edmund Greenleaf, widow of Henry Somerby. The descendants of this marriage of Tristram, Jr.'s, have ever since occupied this fine old mansion which Somerby had left her, or her father, Captain Greenleaf, bestowed.

Edward Starbuck had come over from Derbyshire in 1640, and established himself at Dover. Elder of the Church and Representative, he became a Baptist, and soon after a Quaker. Both he and Thomas Macy are said to have been among the chief promoters of the settlement of Nantucket.* It was no doubt often discussed, and perhaps slowly brought about. Nantucket, an island fifteen miles by four, embracing an area of about thirty thousand acres, lay at the southern extremity of what is now Massachusetts. It was then part of New York, and so remained till 1692. When the project was ripe, and it was concluded to purchase, Tristram, early in 1659, made a voyage of inquiry and observation to the group of islands off the Massachusetts coast with this view. He first visited Martha's Vineyard, whither Thomas Mayhew (1591-1681-90), formerly a merchant in Southampton in England, had, in 1647, removed from Watertown to preach to and convert the Indians. The name of his first wife, Martha Parkurst, he doubtless gave to the vineyard where he so long dwelt gathering souls from the heathen.

---

* Fifteen miles by eleven in the widest part, and twenty miles south of the peninsular of Cape Cod, 120 miles S S E of Boston. Latitude 41° 13' to 41° 21' N, longitude 69° 56' to 70° 13'. Population, 1820, 7,266. In 1824 Sir Isaac was there; in 1826, 352 vessels engaged in the fisheries, 2,392 in the coasting trade, entered its port. This was before the era of steam. —Lieber's Enc. Am.

We are inclined to believe, though we have no conclusive proof, that the attention of Tristram was first called to Nantucket by Mayhew, and the question suggests itself whether it had not been from consanguinity that Mayhew proposed or urged the settlement. He held, in 1649, a conveyance of Nantucket, as he did of Martha's Vineyard, from Lord Sterling. Born in 1591, Petronel Boscawen, sister of Mary, may have been his mother or grandmother. That Mary Boscawen was Tristram's great-grandmother seems more than probable. Southampton, by sea, is not far from Plymouth. It is the seaport of Wiltshire. Mayhew named two towns on the Vineyard from places in that county.

Mayhew and Mayhowe bear the same arms, and are corruptions or variations of the same name. If Thomas Mayhew, born 1591, was son or grandson of that Petronel Boscawen, sister of Mrs Peter Coffin, who married Peter Mayhowe, as mentioned in Collins, Mayhew would have been kinsman of Tristram not remote. Whether this be so or not, Thomas Mayhew, having procured for himself and son, in 1641, from Lord Sterling and Sir Ferdinando Gorges, conveyances of both the islands, Martha's Vineyard and Nantucket, eighteen years later (July 2, 1659) conveyed Nantucket to Tristram Coffin and his associates, reserving about a tenth part for himself. He sent Peter Folger, grandfather of Benjamin Franklin, who had come with him from Watertown, and was familiar with the Indian languages, with Tristram to explore. Tristram, soon after reaching Nantucket, purchased of Potinot, an Indian sagamore, the island of Tuckernuck, at its westerly end, containing a thousand acres

Whether James Coffin came with his father, Tristram, at that time, or later in the fall with Thomas Macy, Edward Starbuck, and Isaac Colman, after his father's return to Salisbury, is not clear, but James remained through the winter on the island as they did. May 10, 1660, the sachems of Nantucket conveyed to the associates for £80 a large part of the island, Peter Folger being witness.

IV.

NANTUCKET.

EARLY in 1660, Tristram, with his family, came to Nantucket. Possibly some delay took place, as regarded them, in providing habitations. It was not long, however, before enough of the settlers and their families had arrived for their security and to plant their crops. Besides Tuckernuck, the Coffins had thus a quarter of the island, and much more in the sequel became theirs. Tristram took the lead from the first among the settlers, and was frequently selected to transact important public business. His letters to the colonial government of New York, of which province Nantucket was then a dependency, are preserved in the archives of the Department of State at Albany.

Although from the earliest settlement regarded as their leader and head by his associates, his first appointment by the Governor at Albany as chief magistrate of Nantucket was as early as 1671. Thomas Mayhew held the like office at the Vineyard. These officials, with two assistants from each island, constituted a general court, with appellate jurisdiction over both. This court sat in each island alternately, its chief magistrate presiding. In 1677 he succeeded Thomas Macy as the chief, and we find on the records of Nantucket an official oath of his, which reads as follows:

"Whereas I, Tristram Coffin Senior, have received a commission dated the 16th of September 1677 investing me with power to be Chief Magistrate on the Island of Nantucket and its dependencies for the four years ensuing, under further order, I, Tristram Coffin aforesaid do engage myself under the penalty of perjury to do justice in all causes that come before me according to law, and endeavor to my best understanding, and hereunto I have subscribed—"

TRISTRAM COFFIN
Chief Magistrate.

Subscribed before
his son Peter.
William, John
and Stephen
being his bondsmen.

Exemplary in his own habits, Tristram respected the rights of other men to regulate their lives according to the dictates of their own consciences, where not conflicting with the law. When in the inn he had established by the Merrimack, for the convenience of travellers over the ferry, complaint was made that threepence was charged the quart for beer instead of two as stipulated in the license, which required four bushels of malt to the hogshead, his wife, through the brewer, proving that she put in six bushels, it was dismissed. At Nantucket, where there were, according to tradition, two or three thousand Indians, under their several sagamores, their proclivity to stronger beverages degrading and brutalizing, led to frequent disputes among themselves, and aggressions upon the settlers, then a mere handful compared with their own numbers. The court records are largely occupied with the trials and sentences of Indians to be whipped for intemperance, or for offences growing out of it. Repressive laws, one drawn up by Tristram, were not without effect. Thomas Macy, in a letter in 1776 to Governor Lovelace, at Albany, states that they had been attended with good results That same year John Gardner, whose gravestone is that of the earliest date remaining, complains to Dudley that his own stock had been seized by Macy, and says that the sachems declare they will fight if the law is enforced.

The manifest improvement in the habits both of the red man and the white was no doubt due in a large measure to other influences than the severities of the law. Tristram, as the wealthiest of the proprietors, used his means generously for the common advantage. If mills to grind the corn, harrows, or other implements of agriculture were needed, it was he who furnished them. When the Indians grew restless and menacing, he held them in subjection and peace in such manner as commanded their respect. He employed large numbers in his farming operations, and built them on his own land improved wigwams. Benjamin Franklin Folger, one of the best and latest of the historians of the island, in speaking of his relations to the Indians, says the Christian character which he exhibited, and which he practically illustrated in all the various circumstances and conditions of the infant colony, is analogous to that which subsequently distinguished the founder of Pennsylvania, so that the spirit of one seemed but the counterpart of the other.

He had had his trials, but bore them with courage and humility. One has been remembered, which caused him much annoyance and loss. It grew out of an official act which forced him to sacrifice his property, and was one of omission rather than commission A ship was wrecked on Nantucket shoals, in September, 1678, loaded with hides, and the chief magistrate allowed the inhabitants to save the wreckage. Portions of the cargo and rigging were embezzled. A Court of Admiralty held the chief magistrate responsible, and the parties who had derived the benefit of wrecking the vessel refusing to bear any part of the fine, the burden fell upon Tristram Coffyn alone. His own testimony in the case seems to have been all the evidence against him upon which the decision was made up. No one of his descendants will read the story, as officially recorded, without a feeling of pride that their great ancestor, under a most distressing ordeal, in which both his fortune and his honor were at stake, saved his honor. And the Governor of New York discharged him from the award of the Admiralty upon his representation.

Through these documents, preserved for more than two centuries, we get a glimpse of the spirit of the times which our Nantucket ancestors impressed with their own personality And, while the first settlers were not all agreed upon the subjects of public policy which subsequently entered into the political concerns of the island, and while their dissensions oftentimes assumed a degree of acrimony and vindictiveness painful to reflect upon, they were very generally men of sturdy character and heroic lives. Looking back through the dim vista of two hundred years, we shall behold a galaxy of names illumined by high resolves—names that have not tarnished with time, nor faded from the world with the friction of the centuries—names that were not born to die We shall see engraven high up on the world's escutcheon the names of Macy, Starbuck, Folger, Gardner, Swain, Hussey, Coleman, Barnard; and then, still higher up, resplendent with innumerable descending rays of light and love and Christian sympathy, extending throughout the broad universe, we shall see the name of Tristram Coffyn.

In 1661 Tristram lost his mother, Joanna Thember, who died in Boston at the age (1584-1661) of seventy-seven. His daughter Elizabeth, born in England, 1634, died at the age of forty-four, the wife of Stephen Greenleaf.

The very admirable Mary Coffin, born at Haverhill, in 1644, married soon after their arrival at Nantucket, at the age of eighteen, Nathaniel, son of Edward Starbuck. Their daughter Mary was the first European child born on the island. Tristram gave them two hundred acres, near half his own allotment, at Capaum Pond, and there they resided near him about twenty years, till his death. Of noble character and disposition, superior powers, and extended influence, Mary was peerless in all the graces of womanhood, and also an eloquent preacher among the Quakers. Her husband was every way a fitting companion for one so gifted and admirable. Their daily associations with Tristram and his wife, Dionis, must have been a mutual advantage and solace to them. She died in 1717, at the age of seventy-two, her husband two years later, at eighty-three.

As Tristram began to feel "the symptoms of a strong man failing," a phrase used by Sir Walter Scott in reply to an inquiry as to his own health, made in the presence of the writer, he disposed of his estate, not by formal testament, but by deeds, the consideration always being his regard and natural affection. He had made large provision for his daughter, Mary Starbuck, and provided homes for those of his other children who needed his aid; he now conveyed most of what remained to his two youngest sons, John and Stephen, to take after the decease of himself and wife In this he followed an ancient practice in England before wills were much in use—disposing of his estate while he lived, reserving the use for life. In the earlier English conveyancing the owner released to the crown, holding the eminent demesne, a new grant being then issued to the new feoffee specifying the terms and conditions previously agreed.

V.

TRISTRAM'S DEATH AND DESCENDANTS

Tristram lived out his four years as Chief Magistrate, and as his term reached its close, his venerable form was borne from his home near Capaum Pond to the graveyard, half a mile away on the ridge. The actual spot can no longer be identified. The earliest stone remaining, that of John Gardner, dates twenty-five years later. Tradition points out a depression in the ground where is said to have stood Tristram's dwelling, another where once existed the Quaker meeting-house, but all around has been long since abandoned for human habitations.

We can easily conjure up that throng of noble men and women, devout and sad, his sons and daughters, their children, friends, and kinsfolk, who accompanied his remains to their last resting-place. But Tristram needs no monument to perpetuate his memory. The thousands and tens of thousands who look back with pride and affection to him, their honored progenitor, multiplying with their generations, will keep in perennial bloom the fragrance of his active and useful life, of his traits and works.

He had had manifold blessings. His mother, Joanna, his wife, Dionis; his sisters, who came over with him from Devon, Eunice, Mrs. William Butler, Mary, Mrs. Alexander Adams, were in every way excellent and devoted. Mary, his seventh child, born in Haverhill in 1645, for nearly twenty years after her marriage, at the age of seventeen, to Nathaniel, the son of Edward Starbuck and Catharine Reynolds, was his near neighbor and constant companion. Mr Allen Coffin justly describes her, in his life of Tristram, when he thus speaks of her

"She was a most extraordinary woman, participating in the practical duties and responsibilities of public gatherings and town meetings, on which occasions her words were always listened to with marked respect. The genius of whatever attaches to the Equal Rights for Women movement of the present day, in every true and proper sense, she anticipated by two centuries, and reduced to practice without neglecting her domestic relations. She was consulted upon all matters of public importance, because her judgment was superior, and she was universally acknowledged to be a great woman. It was not that her husband, Nathaniel Starbuck, was a man of inferior mould that she gained such prominence, for he was a man of good ability; but because of her pre-eminent qualifications that she acquired so good a reputation, whereby her husband's qualifications were apparently lessened. In the language of John Richardson, an early preacher, 'The islanders esteemed her as a judge among them, for little of moment was done without her.' In the town meetings, which she was accustomed to attend, she took an active part in the debates, usually commencing her address with, 'My husband thinks' so and so, or, 'My husband and I, having considered the subject, think' so and so. From every source of information, as also from tradition, there is abundant evidence that she was possessed of sound judgment, clear understanding, and an elegant way of expressing herself, perfectly easy and natural to her.

"At the age of fifty-six, she became interested in the religious faith of the Quakers, or Friends, and took the spiritual concerns of the whole island under her special superintendence. She held meetings at her own house, which are often alluded to by visiting Friends who have written concerning the island's early religious history; wrote the quarterly epistles, and preached in a most eloquent and impressive manner, and, withal, was as distinguished in her domestic economy as she was celebrated as a preacher. Of this department, John Richardson, who preached at her house, wrote 'The order of the house was such in all the parts thereof as I had not seen the like before; the large and bright-rubbed room was set with suitable seats or chairs for a meeting, so that I did not see anything wanting according to place, but something to stand on, for I was not free to set my feet upon the fine cane chair, lest I should break it.' Enough might be written concerning her to make an entertaining volume by itself, which may some time be attempted."

Hon. Peter Coffin, the oldest child of Tristram, born at Brixton in 1631, married Abigail, daughter of Edward and Catharine Starbuck, of Dover, N. H., afterward of Nantucket. Peter was one of the original purchasers of Nantucket, and tradition says the wealthiest of them, owning large mill property. He was a merchant at Dover before the purchase, and subsequently lived at Nantucket, but only for a short time to be considered as domiciled there. He was made freeman in 1666 at Dover, a lieutenant in 1675 on service in King Philip's Indian War, a representative in the Legislative branch in 1672-73, and again in 1679. In 1690 he removed to Exeter, N. H. From 1692 to 1714 he was at different times associate justice and chief-justice of the Supreme Court of New Hampshire, and a member of the Governor's Council. He died at Exeter, March 21, 1715, but most of his life was passed at Dover.

His second child, called the younger Tristram, was born in England in 1632. He married in Newbury, Mass., March 2, 1652, Judith Somerby, widow of Henry, and daughter of Edmund and Sarah Greenleaf. She was born in 1625, and died in Newbury, December 15, 1705. He was made freeman April 29, 1668, and died in Newbury, February 4, 1704, aged seventy-two, leaving one hundred and seventy-seven descendants. He was a merchant tailor, and filled many positions of trust and honor in Newbury. The early records of Newbury bear evidence of his identity with the interests of that town. In the severe ecclesiastical contest concerning Rev. Thomas Parker, of Newbury, Tristram Coffin, Jr., bore a conspicuous part in the interest of Mr. Parker, of whose First Church of Newbury he was deacon for twenty years.

This Tristram built, about 1654, according to the able historian of Newbury, the old Coffin mansion, which has remained in the family to the present day; one of the ninth generation born under its ample roof, Miss Anna I. Coffin, now occupying it. It is said to have been built in 1649 by Henry Somerby, whose widow, it will be remembered, Tristram Coffin, Jr., married. It is one of the few old houses left, and is built around a vast chimney-stack, with spacious fire-places, with windows large and small, opening in pleasant surprises, some on closets and some on staircases, and with walls that, when stripped of their papering not many years ago for the purpose of repapering, were found to display such elegant landscape frescos, with artistic designs of figures and foliage, as were wont to decorate fine residences in the days of the Stuarts. It is a matter of tradition that Tristram Coffyn, Sr., lived in this mansion a short time before his final removal to Nantucket.

Two monuments in the graveyard of the first parish of Newbury, bear these several inscriptions, with epitaphs in verse:

"To the memory of Tristram Coffin, Esq., who having served the First Church of Newbury in the office of a deacon for twenty years, died February 4, 1703-4, aged seventy-two years."

"To the memory of Mrs. Judith, late virtuous wife of Deacon Tristram Coffin, Esq, who having lived to see 177 of her children, and children's children, to the third generation, died December 15, 1705, aged eighty."

If sandy and not very responsive to the plough, Nantucket has been ever famous for its flocks and herds. Its most abundant harvests were nevertheless from the ocean. Even before Tristram passed away, "Lost at Sea" was a frequent epitaph for its dauntless mariners. They possessed many ships of their own; sailed many from other places.

In his well-known burst of eloquence in Parliament, Burke, in 1774, pays just tribute:

"Look at the manner in which the New England people carry on the whale fishery. While we follow them among the tumbling mountains of ice, and behold them penetrating into the deepest frozen recesses of Hudson Bay and Davis Strait, while we are looking for them beneath the Arctic Circle, we hear that they have pierced into the opposite region of polar cold; that they are at the antipodes, and engaged under the frozen serpent of the South Falkland Islands, which seem too remote and too romantic an object for the grasp of national ambition, is but a stage and resting-place for their victorious industry. Nor is the equinoctial heat more discouraging to them than the accumulated winter of both the poles We learn that while some of them draw the line or strike the harpoon on the coast of Africa, others run the longitude and pursue their gigantic game along the coast of Brazil."

Their gigantic game has been almost exterminated, as the buffaloes on the prairie. Other ports have attracted their trade, and the population is now but one-half of what it was in its palmiest prosperity. But its children are not degenerate, though forced to seek other fields for their victorious industry. Everywhere are to be found accomplished ship-masters of its familiar names. William Coffin, who first settled in Boston, as his father Nathaniel, who died in Nantucket (1721) at the age of fifty-five, traversed the sea in command of vessels. The proximity of their ancestral home in Devon to the shores may have implanted in their blood tastes and aptitudes for maritime adventure, which gained strength as they found wider employment on this side the Atlantic.

Gardners, Macys, Bunkers, no less than the Coffins, thus showed the mettle of their pasture. Nor was the invigorating influences of its climate, tempered as it was by the Gulf Stream, confined to its vikings Daughters as well as sons of Dorcas and Damaris won eminence in their various pursuits No more admirable examples of womanhood than Mary Coffin and Dorcas Starbuck have been transmitted for emulation. The Quaker faith, tried by persecution among the Puritans, found elements congenial in the pure, salt air, as in the anxieties and bereavements that attended life on the sea. Nor did they grow up in ignorance. Refinements from civilization beyond the Atlantic had become their inheritance through many generations. Tristram Coffin, Thomas Mayhew, John, his grandson, from the Vineyard, these mothers in Israel themselves exhorted and prayed. Their simple trust, and the amiable disposition which these tenets fostered, fruited in generous deed and noble trait. We must all remember within our own experience men and women, even when separated by place and circumstances from the fold, still bearing unmistakable impress of their insular home, as also of its creed, in the beauty of their lives and well-regulated character.

In such a healthy climate, surrounded by the ocean, leading lives of purity and peace, dauntless afloat, industrious ashore, the whole globe with its waters alike by their voyages made familiar to their ken, it is no marvel that their numbers multiplied, or that the young grew up in physical perfection to transmit their precious inheritance of health and strength and comeliness, of character and intellectual power, not only throughout their favored island, but over the country of which it formed so insignificant a part

It needs but a glance at the precious volume of the Coffins, Ewers, Folgers, and Gardners, to see how rapidly multiplied the races of these early settlers, and how few comparatively were the prolific possessors of the earth, our then progenitors. It presents for study a somewhat unusual example of intermarriages on so small a scale which have not deteriorated the stock.

Among these was Edward Starbuck, who died there, 1690, at the age of eighty-six. His son Nathaniel, who married Mary Coffin, sold his brother-in law, Peter Coffin, his estate at Dover, to accompany his father With him came his sister Dorcas, who married William Gayer; and their daughter, Dorcas Gayer, in the course of events married their cousin, Jethro Starbuck, and her sister, Damaris Gayer, Nathaniel Coffin, son of James. The brother of William Gayer, Sir John,* who died 1710, acquired a large fortune in Bombay, which he divided among his nephew William, son of William, and among his nieces Damaris and Dorcas Their brother died in 1712, in Kent, in England, after marrying his cousin Elisabeth He left his New England property to his sisters and to each a thousand pounds. Peter Folger, in 1663, moved to Nantucket, and his youngest daughter, Abiah, and Josiah Franklin were the parents of Benjamin Franklin, Peter Folger's grandchild. Peter married Judith, daughter of Stephen Coffin, and the intermarriages between the descendants of the early proprietors of the island soon made akin all its inhabitants.

Among others who came was Richard Gardner, eldest son of Thomas,

---

* In London there is said still to exist a chapel erected by Sir John Gayer, Mayor in 1649, somewhat historical from the stand he took in trying times Sir John Gayer, uncle of Mrs Nathaniel Coffin, left fifteen thousand pounds for the nurture and education of students for the ministry in London, but he must be a generation later than the Mayor The Mayor was from South Devon He may have been father of this second Sir John, and William the father of Dorcas and Damaris, Mrs Coffin, and Mrs. Starbuck, to whom Sir John, of Bombay, left considerable estates.

who, in 1624, held office under Conant at Cape Ann. William Bunker, 1650–1712, carried to Nantucket by his mother, Jane Godfrey (whose first husband, George, was drowned, 1658, when she married Richard Swaine), married, 1669, Mary, daughter of Thomas Macy. Richard Pinkham, of Dover, Thomas Coleman, who had come out with Sir Richard Saltonstall, 1599-1682, and who left four sons; John Sanborne, of Hampton, by marriage, 1674, with Judith, daughter of the second Tristram Coffin, became also connected with the island.

VI.

BOSTON AND ISAAC COFFIN.

From Tristram's third son, James, came Sir Isaac. James was Judge of the Common Pleas, and for twelve years of Probate, and when forty years later he passed away, at the age of eighty, he was generally loved and respected. By his wife Mary, daughter of John Severance, one of the earliest settlers of Salisbury, he had fourteen children wedded with six Gardners, with Starbuck, two Bunkers, with Macy, Barnard, Clark, 1721, and Harker. The third son, Nathaniel, 1666-1721, by his wife Damaris, daughter of William Gayer and Dorcas Starbuck, and niece of Sir John Gayer, had four sons and five daughters. William, the eldest son of Nathaniel, born in 1691, in 1722 married Ann, daughter of Francis Holmes, of Boston and South Carolina. This event brought William, grandfather of Sir Isaac, to Boston, where he dwelt in honor and affluence till 1774, father and grandfather of that memorable family among the refugee loyalists who took, some may think, the wrong side in our struggle for independence.

When William Coffin, upon his marriage with Ann Holmes, took up his abode in Boston, the place had become a centre of trade, with nearly twenty thousand inhabitants. The towns along the shore and in the interior depended upon it for garments, and, in part, often for food. It was already metropolitan in fashion and in enlightenment. William's mother, Damaris Gayer, lived on at Nantucket till 1764, reaching the great age of ninety, universally beloved. She had derived a considerable estate, as related, from her uncle, her father, and brother; but she had nine children to provide for. By his own prudence and good sense, and from his wife's inheritance, William soon acquired a competence. He joined the Episcopal Church, and held the position for several years of senior warden of Trinity. His death in 1774, as the war broke out, saved him from witnessing the exile and widespread confiscation that awaited his sons. He had had thirteen children of his own, six of them married, who were also prolific. His children, and children's children, counted up about sixty when he died, about the same number as his great-grandfather Tristram's at his death a century before. But of William's descendants bearing the name of Coffin, all have died out in Massachusetts, and not many remain in England, Canada, or South Carolina.

Nathaniel, second son of William Coffin, born in 1727, graduate of Harvard College, 1744, received, in 1750, an honorary degree at Yale. Brought up a merchant, he was early appointed King's Cashier of the Customs, and acquired considerable property. His wife was Elizabeth Baines, whom he married in 1748. They resided near the corner of Essex Street and Rainsford Lane, in Boston, where John and Sir Isaac were born. The tide of the inner harbor washed up to the garden-walls. Near by, in front, stood the Liberty tree, on the main street, which Nathaniel, the oldest brother of Sir Isaac, cut down in 1774. John, born 1755, after winning great honors by his courage and conduct on the British side in the American Revolution, in its Southern campaigns from 1780 to the peace, died the oldest general in the British Army in 1838. He had three sons and two daughters, and his descendant, Captain Henry Coffin, of the British Navy, published, as we have related, a memoir of him in 1880. One other brother of Sir Isaac, and the youngest, Jonathan Perry, was a barrister of repute in London. His sisters, Elizabeth and Christian, died in 1826, unmarried.

Their sister, Catherine, first married Richard Barwell, of Stansted, distinguished in India, where three of his sons held positions of dignity and trust on the bench, in the treasury, and on the council board. Her second husband was Edward Miller Mundy. Catherine Coffin had only one child by Mr. Mundy, Admiral George, of Holly Bank, Hants, whose distinguished career in the naval service of England in the great war with Napoleon was wise and brave, and gained him great renown. Ann married Mr. Kallbeck.

Isaac, the subject of this memoir, third son of Nathaniel, born in Boston in 1759, at eight years of age—in 1766—entered the Boston Latin School. He was a diligent student in a class that embraced numerous celebrities, and when in Parliament he acknowledged himself indebted to the methods and discipline of the Boston schools for his apt classical quotations, then a mode much in vogue in that august assemblage. His rapid progress and attainments in nautical science, which likewise remain recorded, may have been in some measure due to the mental training of Master Lovell in other branches of learning.

His constitution was, however, too vigorous, his animal spirits too buoyant for scholarship alone to mark his schoolboy days. He led the sports of the playground, and on the fifth of November, the anniversary of the gunpowder plot, was more than once selected as the leader of the burlesque solemnities of the occasion, which was left to the boys of the town for fitting commemoration.

His paternal abode, as mentioned near the corner of what is now Harrison Avenue, at the then south end of the town, was near the Common, and in the frequent battles with foot- or snowball, or with fisticuffs, his activity and strength made him the champion of his party of Southenders, as they were called.

Boston was a pleasant place to dwell in. Its hills, from which it derived one of its names, soon abandoned, rose far higher up above the sea, which then encompassed the thousand acres of land constituting its area. For comfort, security, or easy access to the harbor, the mass of its population clustered about the wharves or centres of trade. Broad stretches of tree or turf, sloping pastures, and blooming gardens surrounded the stately abodes of the wealthy. Tide-waters, fresh from the ocean, spread nearly around the peninsula. Beyond these basins wooded heights of considerable elevation lifted themselves above the boundless tree-tops, delighting the beholder with their graceful proportions. For fishing or shooting, rowing, sailing or swimming, coasting or skating, Boston and its environs of lakes and orchards was then the paradise for boys. It was a capital school for his play-hours, and the old Latin, the oldest school in the country, dating from 1635, for his studies of a graver sort. There fifteen of his cousins were his schoolmates, a host of our own celebrities, and four—Sheaffe, Morland, Mackay, and Ochterlony—who became baronets or generals by military service, at what was then called home. He was well placed for development, nor were his opportunities neglected.

As he grew in wisdom and stature, the ingratitude of king and parliament for the services which had added Canada to the realm created discontent and disaffection. The settled policy of the ministry to subject the colonies to arbitrary rule, to exactions, violating the spirit and letter of their charters, sacrificing their industries for the benefit of merchants and manufacturers at home, provoked resentment, led to eventual resistance and separation. Commercial places, wealthy and intelligent, expressed displeasure through the press, in caucus, and halls of legislation. Conversation and correspondence aroused the people to a sense of their wrongs, and sought to awaken England to the danger of losing so important a part of her dominions. Many, convinced independence must come sooner or later, inflamed the popular passions to bring it about. Others, with more to risk, no less determined in claiming their rights as British subjects, were yet hardly prepared to sever ties sacred from so many associations. They loved the country of their ancestors, took pride in its history, and would have gladly averted the impending calamity.

Loyalists and patriots alike, prompted by honorable motives, grew warm as they discussed the situation wherever men congregated. They were all the more wedded to their own several opinions by the heat and temper such discussion engendered. Liberty boys from the Green Dragon, merchants and officials who addressed Governor Gage, represented the extreme views. But events hurried them on. The Stamp Act, too late and too grudgingly repealed, left its canker. The burning of Hutchinson's costly books and mansion, citizens massacred by British troops, the tea thrown into the ocean, the Boston Port Bill that closed our harbor to navigation, kept at fever-heat the irritation, till twenty thousand of the bone and sinew of the land, from their encampments on its neighboring hills, beleagured the British fleet and garrison; who, after another year, were forced by Washington to withdraw to Halifax. Three thousand of the inhabitants went with them, preferring exile and impoverishment to giving up their allegiance. A few months later the Declaration of Independence at Philadelphia shut with an ominous clang the door against all possibilities of reconciliation.

The Boston Coffins were all loyal to England. Isaac's father held the most lucrative post there under the crown. Their acquaintances and friends were naturally more among the British officers sent to subjugate, than among those conspiring to cast off the yoke. They had much to lose if they swerved from their fealty to the mother country. All this they sacrificed without hesitation for what they considered their obligations. Men act from mingled motives; but now that no object is to be answered by depreciating the loyalists, it seems as unreasonable to condemn them as it would be Roundhead or Cavalier. Isaac was too young in the earliest stages of the turmoil to realize what it meant, but long before he entered, at the age of fourteen, the British navy, he no doubt had formed opinions of his own. It was doubtless of advantage to him, quickening his faculties and maturing his character, that such events were transpiring about him at this plastic period. His sense of justice and right, and of what freedom signified, proved in his subsequent career that these advantages had not been without effect.

His uncles and their sons were all of one mind for the crown. The daughters of the house sided with their husbands, some of whom remained neutral or went with the patriots. They were strong in numbers and near neighbors. Along the principal thoroughfare, its several portions now merged into Washington Street, dwelt twenty families descended from William Coffin, or their near kinsfolk, who lived in constant intercourse. The patriarch, at fourscore, his vigor hardly abated, lived on the main street, near Isaac's home. His daughter Elizabeth had married her cousin, my own progenitor and namesake, who had bought the house opposite her father's, at the corner of Hollis Street, built by Governor Belcher for his own use not long before he went to New Jersey as governor of that province. Mrs. Amory, her own aunt, and the widow of her husband's father, lived farther south on the same street. Her tombstone, marked with her name, lays in the Granary Burial Ground, near Park Street corner, the inscription easily read through the open iron fence surmounting the wall.

Opposite the fence, farther north, at the corner of Bromfield's Lane, where now stands Horticultural Hall, lived another aunt of Isaac, Mrs. Gilbert Deblois, who, if somewhat domineering even for a Coffin, liked to be hospitable. Her boys went also to the Latin school near by. Her cake and fruit were not wasted, but served to rejoice at lunch their healthy appetites. She was less considerate of her pretty daughter, Bessie, who, about the age of Isaac, early became attached to one every way worthy, and whose name in his own and two subsequent generations has been held in high estimation. Why the mother interfered, and forbade the banns in open church, locked up her daughter, whom she seized upon in the act of eloping with her lover, can only be explained by her love of domination. Neither herself nor Bessie could have favored the suit of Arnold, then covered with laurels from Saratoga, later dishonored, who was also captivated by her beauty. Bessie remained single, watching with filial tenderness over the declining years of her mother, who had thus cruelly thwarted her own prospects of a happy life. She lived on, for the most part in the same dwelling, retaining her grace and loveliness till she died, having lived to beyond fourscore, beloved and esteemed by a large circle of acquaintances, friends. and kinsfolk.

Not far from the school, on the Main Street, near the Province House, lived his Uncle William, whose wife was the daughter of Thomas Aston, and who had a large family of sons and daughters. On State, then King Street, opposite the scene of the Boston massacre, resided Mr. Edward Payne, who, disturbed at whist by the turmoil, and hastening, with his cards in his hand, to the door to see what it meant, had his arm shattered by a ball. On what is now Bowdoin Square, with large gardens about it, was the residence of Mr. Newell, Chairman of the Selectmen during the war, who had married a sister of Mrs. Payne, and they were kinswomen of Isaac. John and Eben, his uncles, had their homes near by his own, swarming with children with those best blessings of Providence—good spirits and temper, health, and comeliness. They lived near the Common. These many doors opened gladly to welcome one so cheery and spirited as our subject.

VII.

ISAAC AT SEA.

LIVING surrounded by the sea, sailing on its bays and harbors, and haunting its wharves and ships, Isaac's tastes for maritime pursuits early developed. At the age of fourteen he entered the Royal Navy under the auspices of Rear-Admiral John Montague. By him he was confided to the care of Lieutenant William Hunter, at that period commanding the brig Gaspee, and who thus spoke of his pupil.

"Of all the young men I ever had the care of, none answered my expectations equal to Isaac Coffin. He pleased me so much that I took all the pains in my power to make him a good seaman; and I succeeded to the height of my wishes, for never did I know a young man acquire so much nautical knowledge in so short a time. But when he became of use to me, the Admiral thought proper to remove him. We parted with considerable regret."

Mr Coffin, after quitting the Gaspee, served as midshipman successively on board the Captain, Kingfisher, Fowey, and Diligent, on the Halifax Station; from the latter vessel he was removed into the Romney, of fifty guns, bearing the flag of his patron at Newfoundland, and in the summer of 1778 he obtained a lieutenancy and the command of the Placentia cutter. In the following spring he served as a volunteer on board the Sybil frigate, Captain Pasley, and was soon after appointed to the command of Le Pincon, an armed ship. On this vessel, owing to the negligence of the sailing master who had charge of her, he had the misfortune to be wrecked on the coast of Labrador; upon which he returned to St. John's, where he was tried by a court martial and fully acquitted, his conduct being considered that of an able officer and seaman wholly free from blame.

By following such traces as the naval histories of Great Britain afford of these several ships, we can reasonably conjecture the part Coffin took in our Revolutionary War. We learn what duties were performed by each of them, and we have no reason to doubt, from his rapid promotion, of his efficiency and zeal. We know that his patron, Admiral Montague, protected the rear of Howe's retreat from Boston, in 1776, that the ships to which he belonged were often engaged with the enemy, and that they captured several valuable prizes, in which actions he participated But interesting as this view of the war of Independence is from the decks of English fleets, little comparatively is familiar to American students of their history, or known of Coffin's own experiences to relate them here as incidents in his life.

In November, 1779, Coffin, now lieutenant, went to England and was appointed to the Adamant, about to be launched at Liverpool. In June, 1780, that ship sailed for Plymouth under jury masts; and in the month of August following she was ordered to convoy the trade bound to New York. His next appointment was to the London, of ninety-eight guns, the flag-ship of Rear-Admiral Graves, then second in command on the coast of America, and from her he removed into the Royal Oak, a third-rate, under Vice-Admiral Arbuthnot, to whom he acted as signal lieutenant in the action off Cape Henry, March 16, 1781. As he rose in rank and was clothed with graver responsibilities, the part he took was more conspicuous, and we may mention, even in connection with an officer so young as he was, much of what took place.

The events of the first four years of the war, from 1775 to 1779, are sufficiently familiar; D'Estaing's repulse at Savannah and Prescott's evacuation of Newport in October, 1779; its reoccupation by Tiernay in July, 1780. The reduction of Charleston, defeat of Gates at Camden, defection of Arnold, capture at sea of Henry Laurens, had followed in quick succession. Congress sent, in December, 1780, John, son of its captured president, who had gained glory in the recent battles, to help extricate his father from the Tower, and arrange with King Louis, Franklin, and Vergennes for the coming campaign. Britain, disappointed, had sued for peace by arbitration, which France was disposed to concede on condition of American independence. Meanwhile the King urged his allies to make strenuous exertions to better their condition, which seemed also the English policy, that they might respectively treat to better advantage.

Arnold's sack of Virginia, Cornwallis' march to Yorktown, manœuvred thither by Lafayette, Wayne, and Greene, were preparing the crisis. The King, in March, '81, had promised millions of money, arms, and garments. He provided for the co-operation of De Grasse, with a formidable fleet and several thousand men from the West Indies, with Washington and Rochambeau in the Chesapeake at the end of August.

A French squadron in March, 1781, had a partial engagement at Cape Henry with Admiral Arbuthnot, under whom Coffin, as mentioned, served as signal lieutenant. Washington and Rochambeau in July passed round

New York, reaching the Chesapeake as De Grasse with his twenty-four line-of-battle ships made his appearance. The English leaders, both on land and along shore, had been on the watch, and Graves, Hood, and Drake, with nineteen ships, hovered near. Upon their arrival, De Grasse stood out to sea, the British fleet following. In the engagement of the 5th of September that ensued, the British lost a few hundred men and De Grasse accomplished his object. De Barres, who had come down from Newport, improved the occasion to enter the bay, and the two French fleets thus hermetically sealed it against the British. Graves hurried back to Sandy Hook for reinforcements; but when he returned with seven thousand men, sent by Clinton to relieve Cornwallis, on the 24th of October, it was too late, Cornwallis had already surrendered.

How it chanced that Coffin took no more active part in these operations may be thus explained. After the battle of March 16th, on the return to New York, the Royal Oak, after taking several valuable prizes, had grounded and was sufficiently injured to be hove down at Halifax. In the middle of June arrived a vessel from Bristol with the remains of his father, who had died on board the day before of gout. Having held an important position under government, his obsequies in New York, on Broadway, showed due regard to his memory. Isaac was placed soon after in command of the Avenger, the advanced post of the British up the North River, which he held during the autumn, till he exchanged with Sir Alexander Cochrane for the Pocahontas and joined Hood early in January at Barbadoes.

Lord Hood had been often in Boston. His wife's uncle, Captain John Linzee, had there married the daughter of Ralph Inman, of Cambridge. Lord Hood was present at this marriage, as afterward at that in the same apartment in the house of Mr John Rowe, who had also married an Inman, of Linzee's daughter Hannah to my namesake and father's brother. Under the same roof William H. Prescott, whose wife was the daughter of Hannah Linzee, wrote his earlier histories. Hood well knew Coffin, and it required very little solicitation on his part to invite him to serve on board the Barfleur, his flagship.

Soon after the surrender at Yorktown Hood had sailed for Barbadoes, awaiting De Grasse. January 14, 1782, soon after Coffin had joined him, he learned that De Grasse had relinquished his plan of attacking Barbadoes, and gone to St. Kitts, where De Bouille had landed eight thousand troops, the British garrison under Frazer consisting of but six hundred men.

Deciding to attack the French fleet at anchor to save the place, Hood embarked Prescott, who had twice been in command at Newport, with the few troops that could be spared from Antigua, and set sail. At daybreak he signalled for battle, but the Alfred, running foul of the Nymph, arrested the prosecution of the design, in order to repair damages De Grasse put to sea to have more room to manœuvre, and thus secure the advantage of his superiority in numbers. At daylight on the 25th, the French fleet, twenty-nine sail strong, formed in line of battle three leagues to leeward Hood, who had but twenty-two, pushed the enemy still farther to leeward while he took possession of Basse Terre, the position Hood had left. The Count, astonished at these excellent operations which cut him off from his army, made a furious onset on the British rear, commanded by Affleck, who, under an incessant fire, covered the ships till they reached their several stations.

The next morning the French admiral attacked again the British, van and rear, but was repulsed, losing a thousand men. His own flagship, the Ville de Paris, present of that city to the King, all the next day lay upon her heels covering her shot-holes. The siege proceeded with various success, till De Bouille arrived with four thousand fresh troops, when Frazer capitulated. Hood, on the 19th, reached Antigua, and joined, a few days later Lord Rodney, with reinforcements from England.

These operations form an epoch in the annals of the British Navy. Compelling an enemy of a superior force to quit his anchorage, taking himself the situation thus left during action, defeating every attempt to force the position, and cutting the enemy off from his army. It was a lesson in naval tactics that will ever be deservedly regarded with admiration, both for Hood's skill in these masterly manœuvres, and for the bravery and precision with which they were executed by those under his orders.

While at Santa Lucia, Rodney, learning that De Grasse, with 5,500 men and heavy guns, had pushed for St. Domingo to reduce it, overtook him on April 7th, and the battle of the 9th and victory of the 12th were the results The battle on the 12th began at seven in the morning. It was fought in a large basin of water lying among the islands of Guadaloupe, Dominique, the Saints, and Marie Galante. Both on the windward and leeward of this bay lay dangerous shores. As day broke, Rodney closed up his line at one cable length instead of at two, as usual, each ship as she ranged up to her opponent giving and receiving a tremendous fire. At noon, with his own ship, the Formidable, and three more, he bore down upon the enemy within three ships of the centre and broke through. His other ships followed, doubling upon the enemy and placing them between two fires. Rodney then wore and signalled the van to tack, they gained the windward and completed the disorder and confusion of the French.

The French continued the combat, attempting to reform their broken line by the van breaking away to windward. Meanwhile Hood, in the Barfleur, earlier becalmed, rushed down upon the foe. The Canada, 74, took the Hector. Ingrefield in the Centaur attacked the Cesar; the captain nailed his colors to the mast and was killed. When she struck her mast went overboard, and she had not a foot of canvas without a shot-hole. The Glorieux fought bravely, but was forced to yield. The Ardent was retaken, the Diadem, 74, went down by a single broadside attributed to the Formidable, Rodney's flag-ship.

Between the French ship, the Ville de Paris, and the Canada, a desperate action raged for two hours. De Grasse seemed determined to sink rather than strike. The Barfleur, Hood's flag-ship, on which was Coffin, at sunset poured in a fire which killed sixty men outright, and De Grasse struck to Hood. It is said that at the time she struck but three men were left alive and unhurt on the upper deck, and the Count was one.

Hood, despatched in pursuit of the French vessels that attempted to escape, overtook and captured four. The whole loss of the French amounted to eight vessels, one of which was sunk and another blown up. On the Ville de Paris were thirty-six chests of money to pay the troops. She was said to have been at that time the only first-rate ever carried into port by any commander of any nation. The French lost 3,000 men, the British 1,000. Rodney was made a peer of Great Britain, Hood of Ireland, Drake and Affleck baronets

VIII.

CAPTAIN OF A SEVENTY-FOUR.

SHORTLY after the battle of April 12, 1782, Captain Coffin, who had rejoined his sloop, went with part of the crew of the Santa Amonica, which had been wrecked at Tortola, to Jamaica, where, through the influence of Hood, he was appointed by Lord Rodney captain of the Shrewsbury, of 74 guns, and confirmed in that rank June 13, 1782, sixty days later, when only twenty-two years of age. This indicates the estimate of both Hood and Rodney of his ability, prudence, and courage, of the value of his services in these recent operations.

While still in command of the sloop Pocahontas at Antigua, the town of St. Johns caught fire and in a short space was nearly consumed. Coffin, with the crew of his sloop and other sailors collected by his exertions, at length succeeded in arresting the progress of the flames, at the imminent risk of his life. For this service he had the satisfaction of receiving an address of thanks from the legislative body of the island

It is not easy to determine, from the varying accounts of these battles, whether Coffin, on April 12, 1782—Rodney's great victory—was on board the Barfleur with Hood, or in command of his own vessel Soon after that event we find him despatched on special service, to carry a portion of the crew of the above ship, as just stated, the Mona Amonica, which had been captured September 14, 1779, by his friend, George Montague, in the Romney, to Jamaica. Forming part of the operations, in which he shared with the rest and gained his promotion, this brief sketch of these events will not seem out of place. Great sea-fights before and since—Trafalgar, St. Vincent's, and many more—have displayed the naval genius of great commanders, when seamanship and bravery have won glory for Britain.

In these encounters the great embarrassment to contend with was less the enemy than the wind. This is now changed. The development of steam-power, not only for propulsion, but armor and armament, has brought to an end the naval tactics which controlled the result in engagements where combatants were well matched. Ships, clad like the warriors of old in complete steel, now set at defiance wind and tide.

Since the Monitor, they have effectually superannuated the wooden walls to which nations old and new once trusted for safety and supremacy. If no longer ships by thousands participate in the decisive battles of the future, contending fleets, composed of vessels of great cost, fewer in number, hurling their huge missiles out of sight to their target, will change the whole character of naval warfare. If we have no fleet, to speak of, of our own, we spend millions in feeding useless mouths without benefit to the nation. It behooves us to educate our officers to become Nelsons and Collingwoods, Porters and Farraguts, when circumstances not to be foreseen or controlled, forces upon us another Salamis.

Unless we guard our cities with the latest improvements in defensive warfare, possess fleets able to cope with the best, we may be exposed to tribute, to aggression, or insult—have left no alternative but the last argument of kings and nations, the arbitrament of arms. Sir Archibald Allison, thirty years ago, from his reading of human history, that inasmuch as mankind always fought when they could afford it, predicted that the precious metals discovered in such heaps would reopen the gates of Janus. The event has justified his prophecy. It is to be hoped that the growing intelligence of the race will recognize the absurdity of spending blood and treasure in such profitless avocations. Yet, while the world continues ignorant and stupid, we should be prepared for attack. We should have forts, ships, and captains, who will learn from the old strategy and tactics, on land and sea, what they had of value—accomplished commanders, who can, besides, devise new methods to meet the modern facilities of destruction, which science, like Cadmus of old, who invented the alphabet, brings out of the earth.

Peace soon came. Though Coffin had gained a permanent rank in the Navy, there was much to discourage him in finding his vocation thus changed, if not gone. His family was broken up. The remains of his father lay in their last resting-place, as already mentioned, in New York. John, at the age of twenty-one, had raised a mounted rifle corps in New York called the Orange Rangers, which, with him as their commandant, took part in the battle of Long Island, August 27, 1776, and in that of Germantown, October 4, 1777. Later, he exchanged into the New York Volunteers, was at San Lucie and Brier's Creek in 1779, at Camden in 1780, at Holkirk's Hill, near Camden, April 25th, and at Eutaw Springs September 8, 1781. He is mentioned, as a brave and successful cavalry officer, with commendation in nearly every other engagement of the Southern campaign, constantly in desperate encounters and coming off victorious. Though a purse of ten thousand dollars was offered for his capture, he escaped to Charleston, where he married, as the war closed, Miss Matthews, and establishing himself later on his manor of Alwington, on the St John's, in New Brunswick, he lived till he was eighty-two in great honor. That at the close of the war of Independence, at the age of twenty-seven, his rank was only that of a major, that he was not promoted to a higher rank, as urged by Howe and Cornwallis, is attributed to enmity at court for telling the truth of a favorite. He was at the head of the generals when he died

As he has had recently (1880) his biographer in one of his descendants, Captain Henry Coffin, of the Royal Navy, this is not the place to relate more particularly his brilliant achievements or numberless anecdotes well remembered. I vividly recall his tall commanding figure and marvellous bright eyes, in my early home in Park Street, in Boston, where he was a frequent visitor of my father, who had charge of his affairs as of his brother's He was more sedate than Isaac, but both were brilliant specimens of the race. He was beloved and greatly esteemed by his numerous cousins, and splendid salmon from the river near his home were often sent by him for their enjoyment. He also, like his brother, if not on so grand a scale, in order to promote our stock, sent fine horses to the Agricultural Society at Brighton.

The brothers, of nearly the same age, and the best of friends, Isaac may well have wished to have been present at John's wedding to Miss Matthews, which took place toward the close of 1782. Charleston lay on the route from Antigua, and it would not have been strange if, in the spirit of mutual consideration that prevailed in the service, such an opportunity had been given him. If so, it does not appear.

IX.

PEACE OF 1783.

EARLY in 1783, war over, and the Shrewsbury paid off, Coffin exchanged into the Hydra, and going home, was put out of commission. His previous visits to England had been brief and on professional duty. This new experience to one who, at the age of twenty-two, had gained the rank of captain, and by his valuable services made his mark as one of the best officers of the Navy, might have turned the head of one less sensible

To be his own master, with abundance of prize money, plenty of companions, like dashing blades to share it, must have been replete with gratification. Many of his family and friends from Boston had taken up their abode in London, and the refugee loyalists formed there a large circle. They were all disposed to like Isaac, a handsome young fellow with pleasant ways, generous and unpretending, loaded with laurels. If the highest honors of the war attached to superior rank and more distinguished command, he had done enough to be held in estimation among his own intimates, by the great naval celebrities, and by the public.

He was much in France while thus on furlough. Paris still retained the glamour of the old regime. If heavy taxes or arbitrary power created widespread discontent and disaffection, there were as yet few indications of the caldron seething beneath, soon to overwhelm. It is much to be wished more of his correspondence had survived to give us his own impressions of Paris then. He wrote well and with the vivacity that characterized his conversation. Possibly many more of his letters may exist of all periods of his life, and if so, they should be collected.

Sir Guy Carleton, who could hardly have saved Canada for the crown, in 1775, without the aid of the Coffins, and whose private secretary throughout his career was Isaac's cousin, Sir Thomas Aston Coffin, was now, in 1786, appointed Governor of Canada. It was probably at his request that Isaac was appointed to the Thisbe, to take him with his family and suite to Quebec. He had been created Lord Dorchester, that being an old title in the Carleton family. The ship arrived at Quebec late in the season, and, lest she should be frozen up, Coffin proceeded, two days later, to Halifax for the winter, returning in the spring to Canada, and remained there for some months.

At this time a circumstance occurred to disturb his serenity, though later he was entirely exonerated from any blame. It had been long the custom in the English naval service, among other abuses working occasional injustice and demanding reform, to retain on the ship rolls the names of young officers while pursuing their studies ashore; so that they might not, while qualifying themselves for their responsible duties, lose their precedence for promotion. Many years before, in consequence of some unfair advantage that had been taken of this indulgence, a regulation prohibiting such practices had been adopted by the Admiralty. It chanced at this very time someone again had been aggrieved, and attention been called to the prevalence of what had been prohibited. It was ascertained that two such cases were on the rolls of the Thisbe, not placed there with the knowledge of Coffin, but which it was his duty as captain to have discovered and struck off. Upon inquiry and complaint he was suspended, and indignant at what he conceived unfair treatment, he proceeded to Flanders, and entered into the service of the Brabant patriots then in arms against Austria.

This decree of suspension by the board, when appealed from to the twelve judges, was by them declared illegal on the part of the Admiralty and set aside. This put an end to the suspension and restored him to his standing in the service. Upon the Spanish armament in 1790, on the Nootka Sound dispute, he was appointed to the Alligator, and in the following spring, having received the flag of Commodore Cosby, was ordered to America, whence he returned home with Lord Dorchester and his family the following autumn.

While thus stationed at Halifax, he visited Quebec on furlough, and remained there a twelvemonth. He naturally found the place attractive socially as in other ways. Besides his cousin, Thomas Aston, son of his uncle William, his Uncle John resided in that city with his family, who were about his own age. John, early after the outbreak of hostilities at Boston, had taken his wife, Isabella Child, and eleven surviving of his fifteen children, six sons and five daughters, in his own ship, the Neptune, to Quebec. He there purchased land, and when Montgomery and Arnold arrived in December, 1775, to besiege the city, he remodelled the buildings he was constructing for another purpose into a fortification. This he armed with guns from a vessel frozen in for the winter, and with Bainefare, its captain, stood ready with a small force to oppose the assailants. With the first volley he slew Montgomery and his two aids, on the last day of the year 1775, as they attempted to take his fort by assault. This, with Arnold's subsequent loot of Montreal, which disaffected the Canadians, saved Canada for the British crown.

The sons of John all reached distinguished rank in the British civil and military service, and three of his daughters were connected with it by marriage. Isabella married Colonel McMurdo, whose sons gained distinction in India ; Susannah, Hon John Craigie, provincial treasurer, whose son, an admiral, died in 1872 at Dawlish ; his daughter Margaret, Sir Roger Hailes Sheafe, born in Boston, who for his victory at Queenstown Heights, October 13, 1812, was made a baronet One of the sons of John, Francis Holmes, in the navy throughout the war with France, served with distinction and died an admiral in 1835.

While on his way up the river to Quebec in 1786, the Thisbe was becalmed off the Magdalen Islands in the St. Lawrence, and struck by their appearance, perhaps the more attractive from the autumnal splendors, Coffin requested, probably not in very serious earnest, that Lord Dorchester, as representative of the crown, would bestow them on him. This request seemed reasonable to the governor. It was not received at first with favor at home, but renewed the following year in more formal manner, was eventually granted The letters-patent were not expedited until 1798, during the governorship of Robert Prescott. In his will Sir Isaac entailed these islands on his nephew, John Townsend Coffin, and his sons, John's brother, Henry Edward, his cousin William, and several other branches of his own name, and then on the Barwells, his sister's sons The son of Sir Isaac Tristram, who died in 1872, now holds them.

After his return to Europe, while lying at the Nore during a heavy gale, a man fell overboard, and Coffin leaped after him into the sea and succeeded in saving his life. He sustained by his efforts a serious injury, which frequently afterward reminded him of this act of humanity.

Another heroic act, of somewhat similar character, has been related of his promptness in emergencies. While at Portsmouth, or some other naval station, and, it is believed, still a subaltern, his ship, one of the line, caught fire, which being in close proximity to the magazine, sailors and marines rushed with precipitation to the gangway to escape the instantly expected explosion. By authority, or example, he changed their purpose, and the men going to quarters, saved the ship.

Soon after his return the Alligator was paid off. After visiting Sweden, Denmark, and Russia he returned home upon the troubles with France, and in charge of the Melampus frigate was employed on Channel service to the close of 1794. While exerting himself on a boisterous night, when the frigate was in great danger of destruction, he sustained a similar injury to that at the Nore, which compelled him to leave his ship, and for some time he remained a cripple. Nine months later, however, while recovering his strength at Leith on service, he was sent as resident commissioner of Corsica, and remained till October, 1796, when the island was evacuated. From Elba he was removed to Lisbon to take charge for the next two years of the naval establishment at that place. He was thence despatched to superintend the arsenal at Port Mahon when Minorca fell into the hands of the English, and from there ordered to Nova Scotia in the Venus frigate. At Halifax, and afterward at Sheerness, as resident commissioner, he was employed till April, 1804, when appointed rear-admiral he hoisted his flag on the Gladiator on duty at Portsmouth, and the following month he was created a baronet. The record recites the grant of the Magdalen Islands in the St. Lawrence, for his unremitting zeal and persevering efforts in the public service. He was promoted four years later to the grade of vice-admiral, which ended his naval duties afloat, though he became full admiral in 1814 by regular seniority.

This sketch of his services at sea is very incomplete. The memoir of him in 1822, by Marshall, in London, when he was in Parliament, is brief, and the obituary in *The Gentleman's Magazine* when he died, not even as extended. I have no data of his cruise in the Pacific, along the shore of Australia, mentioned by Mr. Allen Coffin, which has left its trace on the charts in Sir Isaac's Point and Coffin's Bay. It seems more likely to have taken place about the close of the last century or the beginning of this.

His prize money in such troubled times had been considerable. This he entrusted to my father, one of his cousins in his native place, favorably circumstanced, to invest it to advantage, and it was said that the income finally equalled the original deposits. He made frequent visits to his early home in the course of his busy life upon the sea, having made more than thirty voyages to and from America.

X.

MARRIAGE AND PARLIAMENT.

AFFLUENT and a baronet, he naturally longed for a home and inclined to transmit his baronetcy to his posterity. March, 1811, he married Elizabeth Browne, the only child of William Greenly, of Titley Court, in Herefordshire. Her family, brought up with rigid notions of propriety, did not take kindly to the hearty and jovial ways which characterized naval officers, and the match proved less happy than expected.

It is said that on one occasion, returning to Titley Court on some particularly festal day, he ordered the sexton, as he passed through the village, to ring a merry peal and send the tenants to the mansion to drink a glass of ale. This mortally offended the lord of the manor, who thus found his prerogative invaded by the husband of his only child. Within a few years, satisfied of their utter incompatibility of temper, they very amicably, on both sides, arranged for independence of each other.

Without intending to detract from her merit, the lady indulged in literary tastes of a religious tendency. She was said to be addicted to writing sermons at night, to the disturbance of the slumbers of her rollicking spouse, and so, after a space they separated. She remained Lady Greenly and he resumed the name of Coffin. The fault was certainly not hers, who was a clever and exemplary woman, but somewhat eccentric in her ways. In after life she was well known in Bath, England, remarkable for wearing, Welsh-woman fashion, a man's round hat, a riding habit cut short, and for wielding a gold-headed cane. She lived nearly as long as he did, but they rarely met, though he made repeated overtures to reconciliation, some rather amusing.

When shipwrecked in the Boston, struck by lightning on her way from Charlestown to Liverpool in 1829, in the boat for several days with little hope of rescue, for the seas were not then as much traversed as now, he expressed great affection for her, and gave his watch to the captain to send her should he himself not survive their perils and the captain be fortunate enough to escape. While in the crowded boat, on this occasion, with no shelter and little covering, and the scantiest supply of food and water, his own cheerfulness, interesting conversation, and ebullitions of good humor, kept his companions in heart and courage.

It is the reasonable ambition of all Englishmen whose conditions and circumstances justify such aspirations, to be permitted to take part in the legislation and government of their country, and when his own health and the peace rendered active service in the Navy no longer desirable, his wish was gratified by his return to Parliament. One of his friends, Lord Darlington, had influence enough to secure his return in 1818, for the borough of Ilchester, for which he sat till the dissolution in 1826. His reputation and experience gave especial weight to his opinions when he took part, as he frequently did, in debates on naval affairs. What he said attracted attention to its practical good sense by the hilarity of his nature and happy stores of illustration that amused while they convinced. He was tall, robust, but of symmetrical proportions; his voice powerful, and his countenance expressive and noble. His long habits of command and contention with the elements inspired confidence in himself, which commanded that of the House. He was widely known and generally popular, and happily constituted to enjoy the social pleasures attending success, tempered in their indulgence by occasional twinges of gout.

Among affluent and influential circles, nowhere more than in England, does the social board shape public opinion, develop and test ability, or even control affairs. This was more the case half a century ago than since reform bills have opened the door more widely to popular representation. Officials and legislators were exclusively selected from rank and wealth, or for extraordinary ability and statesmanship, and the aristocracy they represented regarded the government as their especial concern. Much could be said in the privacy of social discussion which would have been wholly impolitic through the press, or in the halls of legislation. From memoirs and biographies since published, what took place behind the scenes has come to light to show how, and by whom, public affairs were conducted and managed. Many wise and noble statesmen were among the leaders, but much has transpired that had better have been consigned to oblivion. Social chat at the table was not altogether political; it embraced every conceivable topic, and the brilliant encounters of wit, the profound speculations of philosophy, the flood of anecdote and historical reminiscence, contributed to the intellectual banquet.

From his varied opportunities and confidential acquaintance with men and affairs, few had more to impart to the general entertainment of the hour than Sir Isaac. He possessed rich stores of the information most valued, and his jovial nature was contagious and irresistible. In the brilliant round of London hospitalities, in the happily-ordered routine of country life, where scores of able men met in the easiest freedom from constraint as guests together, he was everywhere an acquisition I remember well weeks passed under the same roof with him when preparing for my college examinations. The family were in the country, and he was tied by the foot to his couch by the gout. But from morning till night, droll stories, amusing incidents, whimsies and oddities of every description, exploded like fireworks from the aged man's pillow, intermingled with occasional garnish of more savage intensity at his anguish

XI.

GENIAL TEMPERAMENT.

I HAVE still a vivid recollection of him in his undress uniform as a British admiral, at an earlier period, in fine health and the perfection of physical maturity, on the wide lawn and in the spacious parlors of Belmont, his cousin's and my uncle's home. He was then tall and erect, with rich color in his cheeks and merry sparkle in his eye, brimming over with animal spirits, companionable, and with fitting chat for all. His funny words and ways were the delight and dread of the children, into whose frolics he entered with zest, bewildering their minds with his drolleries, both they and himself exploding with merriment at practical jokes too good-natured to offend.

If not quite as prone to loud expressions of mirth and merriment in social intercourse on this side the ocean as on the other, one so gay and so brimful of amusing jokes and stories was perhaps all the better appreciated. The many brilliant gentlemen of Boston in professional life, or among its merchant princes, affluent and convivial, were pleased to have him as their guest. Loyalty to the mother-country died out slowly, and a Boston-born boy, whose numerous kinsfolk had ample means for hospitality, much attention was paid him. Often when at my father's, who resided in Park Street, where now is the Union Club House, the festal entertainments extended into the small hours, and those upon whom it devolved to sit up to receive the roisterers, would gladly welcome from far off his shout of " House ahoy!" breaking on the silent watches of the night.

While at some lordly mansion in England his hostess had begged him to have made for her a Boston rocking-chair Not wishing to disoblige her ladyship, he enlisted the services of the village carpenter, and a few days after had the contrivance, not then to be found in fashionable mansions out of the nursery, placed in the apartment where the company at the castle assembled before dinner. With all due ceremony he led the amiable and much-honored lady to the chair, in which she ensconced herself and began to rock Unfortunately, the rockers had not been constructed on scientific principles, and over it went, with many eyes to behold. Too well bred to be affronted, she gathered herself up as best she could; and by taking it kindly put the admiral at his ease, and contributed to the gayety of the repast. Her husband, whose good services placed him in Parliament, did not abate them for the casualty.

One day an American ship sailed into Portsmouth, or Plymouth, before the War of 1812, when Sir Isaac had charge of the naval fleet. An English officer was sent on board. The master having gone ashore, the mate, being in charge, did not receive the officer with the etiquette required upon such occasions. The officer gave the first salutation as he reached the deck by saying: "What damned kind of a Yankee lubber has charge here, who don't know his duty to properly receive his majesty's officer?" The mate said not a word, but, seizing his visitor by the collar and slack of his trousers, threw him overboard for his own crew to pick up. Soon after an armed boat came alongside to take the mate on board the flag-ship, where he was arraigned before Sir Isaac, who soon became aware that the culprit was a kinsman, whose father he had been familiar with in boyhood. He tried to get the mate to acknowledge that he was ignorant of the laws and customs, that he might dismiss the case with a caution not to do so again; but the Yankee was obdurate. "He'd be damned," he said, "if any man should insult him on his own deck and under the flag of his country." The offender was remanded to be regularly tried the next day. In the meantime the admiral sent a messenger to privately assure the mate that a suitable apology would relieve him from any further trouble in the matter; but on the trial the same defiant manner was assumed. The admiral drew out some expression, however, which he accepted as satisfactory, and dismissed the offender with suitable admonitions.

Later in the day, from the shore, the admiral sent a message to the young man, stating that, as his father was an old friend and relative, he would be happy to meet the son and enjoy a bottle of wine with him at the inn. But the young man replied that the admiral might go to h—l with his wine. He'd see him d—d first, before he'd drink with any d—d Englisher, especially one who would approve of an insult to an officer under his own flag, upon his own deck.

The admiral used to relate the above incident with much gusto, as he admired the spirit of independence exhibited by the Yankee mate. We have retained the strong garnish, as a fair sample of the profane ways of a few generations ago. Not only afloat on the quarter-deck and on the forecastle, but in the drawing-room and social circles, among those who should have known better, such modes of speech prevailed. They have long since vanished from among all classes and conditions here and throughout christendom.

Commodore Hull, of our Navy, was one of his correspondents, and General Wilson, our honored president, has been good enough to permit me to read many letters that passed between them after the War of 1812, and when the two countries were at peace. This correspondence displays alike in both the genial and generous traits which the Navy is thought peculiarly to foster. I propose to refer to one subject more than once mentioned in these letters, which, to use the old phrase, might seem only a fish story and for the marines, if not evidently believed by himself. It is in reference to the size attained in former days by lobsters on our coasts. In the freedom of intercourse around the table or on the quarter-deck, while once returning to America, he alleged that lobsters had been found weighing ninety pounds. Though given somewhat to rhodomontade, he seems in this instance to have believed the fact based on hearsay, if not on sight. My own fishmonger told me that within his experience in these waters twenty-five pounds was the largest that had come to his knowledge, but I have seen it stated that lobsters of much larger weight have been found down East, where there is more room for expansion and imagination. The size attained by turtles and other shell-fish in neighboring waters renders such possibilities less incredible.

Apropos of Hull and Sir Isaac, my friend, General Wilson, in a recent address on Commodore Hull and the frigate Constitution, said: "When in the presence of a Boston-born British admiral another naval officer indulged in laudatory and extravagant comments on the capture of the Chesapeake and endeavored to underrate the American naval victories of the War of 1812–14, and particularly that gained over the Guerrière, he said, 'It was a lucky thing for your friend Broke that he fell in with the unprepared Chesapeake, and not with Hull and the Constitution. If he had, no Tower guns would have been heard celebrating a Shannon victory.' This manly and patriotic statement was made by Sir Isaac Coffin at the dinner table of the Duke of Wellington, and was related to me by his eldest son, the second Duke, who was present. On the same occasion, when someone spoke sneeringly of the Americans as soldiers, a general of my own name remarked, 'I have been through the Peninsular campaign, and was with the duke at Waterloo, but harder fighting I never saw than we had at Lundy's Lane.'"

XII.

BENEFACTIONS AND DEATH.

Sir Isaac's character was too racy and various not at times to provoke censure or criticism. He did so much that should not be forgotten, so much entitled to be remembered, that, had the time or the occasion allowed, I should mention several anecdotes that have come to my knowledge which show what he was from all points of view. One incident would serve to explain how sometimes he created ill-will by yielding too much to his impulses.

These impulses were quick and generous; his disposition to be of service to his least fortunate kinsfolk he manifested by frequent visits and liberal benefactions, and if occasionally awakening expectations which change of impression or circumstances disappointed, his imperfections as well as his noble traits constituted a part of his character.

I have already mentioned that the judicious investment of his pay and prize-money by one of his cousins had made him rich. In various ways he expressed his gratitude even to another generation. In a paper alluded to in his will he left bequests to a long list of his kindred, many of whom were in straitened circumstances. Others better off he did not forget, bequeathing five hundred pounds to my father's children.

He took an especial interest in the eldest son of this cousin, who had been the junior partner of the house, and been left, by the death of his father, in control. He had married, and taken into the firm one of the best of men, since one of the great house of the Barings of London. Losing his health, Mr. Amory was advised by his physician to go with his wife and children to Europe. When they took their departure, he left Sir Isaac, then his guest, in possession of his dwelling. Sir Isaac had left in the firm, as part of its working capital, $10,000, to be used in its transactions, with the assurance that it should not be called for while he lived. When, owing to some freak of temper to which persons tortured by the gout are liable, he insisted upon having the sum thus lent, and a few thousands more then due, instantly repaid, the brothers and sisters were, for the most part, under age, the paternal property undivided. There existed then no limited liability. Mill corporations recently established, in which his father had largely invested, and of some of which he had been president or director, becoming unproductive, failing, or losing their credit, left exposed the estate, largely composed of land, wharves, and dwellings

It was a most inopportune moment for Sir Isaac to reclaim the loan accepted expressly upon the promise, it should not be called for while he lived. By sacrificing his patrimony in the then depreciated market, Sir Isaac was repaid within the year, though the inheritance of his creditor, thus disposed of, has since been worth twentyfold, at the least, what it brought. This unexpected blow crippled one he had intended to serve, who, with a large family of ten children, struggled on bravely as well as he could without capital, sometimes eminently successful, always active and energetic. Obliging, beloved, and respected, he made the best of his existence ; and if often too sanguine of results, would, but for this, have been as much favored in fortune as he was in his amiable disposition and courtesies. It is too old a story for praise or blame Probably Sir Isaac had forgotten his promise, and when he thought his loan imperilled felt bound to extricate it from danger.

This incident is mentioned not for blame, but explanation. It left at the time an impression to the prejudice of our subject, and as the only blur upon his fame as large-hearted, just, and generous, it should not be misunderstood. Before stocks and bonds offered safe investments for trusts, money was often left with merchants and bankers upon interest, to be used as part of their capital. When the profits of trade judiciously conducted ranged from twenty to thirty per cent., and with little risk, where there was prudence and wealth, houses well established often found it of advantage thus to enlarge their working means. In this instance of uniform and long-continued success and established reliability, hundreds of thousands of dollars were held, some at fixed rates of interest, some receiving a portion of the profits. No corporation existing for the insurance of marine risks, men of property, of various professions and pursuits, visited the offices where such business was transacted, and subscribed as underwriters on ships and cargo. Sometimes people not in trade shared in the ventures of those that were.

In this way the admiral's own fortunes had rolled up, in the care of his cousin, to very respectable dimensions It was with the view of increasing them that he left the loan to be accounted for to his executors with his son and surviving partner. It was not pretended that the loan was used, except in the regular commercial operations of the house. Sudden death, a large family to divide the income, illness that compelled going abroad, led to some delay in responding to the unexpected call for it, and this, where exactness and promptitude had been the unvarying experience, fretted the temper of the admiral. The best of us occasionally act from impulse, and the consequences in the case could not have been foreseen. It is a caution to men not to be precipitate. It prejudiced many of his best friends against him, and no doubt caused him in his later life much regret. But now that nearly half a century has passed, he seems fairly entitled, in the estimation of all, to his place in the calendar free from reproach, so far as this incident is concerned, and the writer knows of no other that is not greatly to his credit.

There is another explanation which, at this day when indulgence in speculation as to motives for transactions so remote can do no harm, may serve to amuse or caution against the possible consequences of similar ebullitions. The admiral had been the frequent guest of his young friend in town and country, using his horses and carriages; and when the family went to Europe, begged him to use his carriage in London, and gave orders to that effect. It so chanced that when about to be presented at court, as there were many other Americans besides to go with them, it seemed the right moment to use the carriage, whose panels were, of course, emblazoned with Sir Isaac's arms. He did not like it, and took it rather in dudgeon, but in this he of course made a mistake.

What bears, also, some connection with the transaction, if not particularly pertinent, may interest some of our readers. Mr. Amory was acting at the Isle of Wight, as representative of Colonel Hunter, our Consul, who had gone over to France for his children, about whose safety there was cause for alarm, when the exiled King and his family having taken refuge in American vessels, placed himself under the protection of our Consulate flag at Cowes. There they remained for several weeks, while the English Cabinet consulted as to how best to receive them. During this period the vice-consul, visiting the King daily on the ship, having the family at his house at Ryde, and occupying their time with excursions about the island, had an interesting experience. He had earlier travelled over Europe, known many of its celebrities intimately, and was always excellent in conversation, and thus able to divert their grief. Sir Isaac may have thought this an extravagance; or, perhaps, was too much of a Liberal in politics to approve these civilities to a monarch so arbitrary.

While a guest at my father's summer house at Newton, he found in the pastor of the church there—Parson Homer—an excellent, learned, but somewhat eccentric clergyman, who had been his schoolmate at the Boston Latin School. The parson, who frequently came to dinner, was apt to be a little long over his grace, to the cooling of the soup. The renewal of their early friendship was a pleasure to both, and the dominie being versed in biblical lore, the admiral added much to the enjoyment of his later years by the gift of a rare and costly Bible, with a letter still extant.

His interest in the school and his classmates never ebbed. His name is found on its books in 1808, the year he was made Master of Arts at Harvard College. Upon his last visit to Boston, not long before he died, he went to the school, then in School Street. One of the then pupils, Dr. Parsons, the peerless translator of Dante, tells me he remembers him well; and that Sir Isaac, with hand upon his head, devoutly invoked a blessing in his behalf.

What remains of his correspondence here is creditable to his good sense, to his ability as a writer, to his broad sympathies. Soon after the war ended, he established in our Massachusetts waters a school-ship for our mates and skippers to learn the art of navigation. The barge Clio, which he purchased for the purpose, was commanded by his kinsman, Captain Hector Coffin, of the Newburyport branch of the name, who was imprudent enough, in 1826, to go up in her to Quebec, flaunting the American flag. These generous projects involved large expenditures, and when his brother, General John Coffin, of New Brunswick, urged him to abandon what gave umbrage at home, he cheerfully acquiesced in giving up what had cost him several thousands of pounds. His desire to be of service to the land of his birth, nevertheless, prompted other beneficent efforts He sent over to Brighton Barefoot, Serab, and several other race-horses that had recently triumphed in the Derby and other well-known courses to improve our breed. He brought over in crates, from English waters, turbot, the first of the European variety in our own, and imported rare fruits and plants for our horticulturists.

These horses, sent out with a groom to take charge of them, were kept in the stables of the Massachusetts Agricultural Society at Brighton. Barefoot had many descendants, Serab, if any, but few. For many years having been the fortunate possessor of one of the Barefoot's colts, it grew up to be perfect for the saddle One day when on his back, an elderly body crossing the street, not having heard the clatter of his hoofs upon the pavement, suddenly changed her purpose, retracing her steps to regain the side she had left. The horse, checked to avoid her, struck his hock against the curb-stone, and was spavined. When broken to the shafts, and left for a moment at the door, he threaded his way through a crowded thoroughfare to the stable-yard, half a mile, without a scratch. It is a pleasure thus to record in print the virtues of that excellent colt whose paternal pedigree was almost as long as that of the Coffins.

He was warmly attached to Nantucket, where his ancestors and their descendants had dwelt for so many generations. He visited the place and became acquainted with his kinsfolk, and in 1826 appropriated twelve thousand dollars (£2,500), afterward increased till now about £10,000, as a fund for a school for the instruction of the posterity of Tristram. This includes nearly every native-born child of the island, besides, perhaps, thousands in every State in the Union, who by future residence may come within its benefits. The Academy still flourishes, though if our present system of public instruction had then reached its present development, his benefactions would probably have assumed another form.

Soon after his mishaps, to which we have already alluded, when burned out of the cotton ship when near Charleston, in 1829, he came to Boston, and when some fresh attacks of his painful disorder induced by the exposure permitted, he hastened back to England.

The Duke of Clarence, William the Fourth, had succeeded his brother George on the throne. His long connection with the Navy attached to him the officers who had grown old with himself. It was said that when the King was urged to create new peers to carry the Reform Bill through the Lords, Sir Isaac was high up on his list as Earl of Magdalen The House of Lords gave in and voted for the Reform Bill, and the proposed new peers were not created Sir Isaac did not long survive his royal friend The 23d of June, 1839, at the age of eighty, he died at Cheltenham, in Gloucestershire, and there he was buried. Lady Coffin preceded him to the tomb on the 27th of January of that year His brother, General John Coffin, died the year before, his death having taken place June 12, 1838, in New Brunswick

Save when in his own cabins afloat, or in his official residences in command of posts, Sir Isaac rarely enjoyed the privilege of a home of his own, unless as such may be regarded his lodgings in London while in Parliament. He found a ready welcome under the roofs of his friends and kinsfolk. His sister, Mrs. Mundy, had a charming abode, Holly Bank, in Hampshire, of which I caught a glimpse when passing its gates, and where another brother of mine and his wife visited her. He had known her sons, the Barwells, pleasantly in India. He chanced to be present, also, at the hotel at Cheltenham when Sir Isaac died. There, and at Bath, where some of his cousins resided, had been his frequent resort, and there he had come to end his days near the family sepulchre.

But I have already exceeded my limit; much omitted may find place in some future publication. I have not aimed at eulogy or indulged in illustration, but simply recited facts that have come to me from diligent study of the subject, many of which had escaped previous investigation. The memory of a Boston boy, who by dint of his own native energy attained the highest rank in the British navy, a generous benefactor whose works still bear witness to the noble impulse that prompted them, thus rescued from oblivion in your publications, may find interested readers not only among his numberless kinsfolk, but even among a larger circle of readers.

The engraving of Sir Isaac which accompanies this memoir is taken from a portrait by Gilbert Stuart, that formerly belonged to his cousin, Thomas C. Amory, on Franklin Place, Boston, and in my earliest recollection hung in the parlor of the house of my aunt, Mrs. Amory, the sister of Admiral Sir Samuel Hood Linzee, cousin of Lords Hood and Bridport. It now forms part of the precious ancestral gallery of my cousin, Mr. William Amory, of Beacon Street, Boston. The portrait in the Coffin School at Nantucket of its founder, by Sir William Beechey, presents Sir Isaac at a later period of life.

XIII.

THE COFFIN COATS OF ARMS.

The Coffins have always claimed coat-armor in hereditary right. That branch descended from Nathaniel Coffin, father of Admiral Sir Isaac, inherit the right through the Admiral's grant, and are unquestionably entitled to wear his coat of arms, but this differs essentially in its emblazonment from the more ancient ones.

Authorities upon English heraldry give, as belonging to the Coffins of Devonshire, a description which, in its combination, is unlike any other family bearings, and consists of bezants and cross-crosslets.

While they differ as to order of arrangement and combination, the number of bezants is never less than three nor more than four, and the cross-crosslets vary from five upward to a semée which is an indefinite convenient number.

The bezants are a roundle representing the ancient gold coin of Byzantium, current in England from the tenth century to the time of Edward III., and was probably introduced into coat-armor by the crusaders. The white roundle exhibited upon Admiral Sir Isaac's arms is of silver, and is usually called a plate, although there were silver bezants used as coin. The cross-crosslets are crosses crossed on each arm.

The crests and mottoes are of quite modern origin.

The six coats of arms in the name in "Burke's General Armory" are as follows.

1. Coffin, Magdalen Islands, Gulf of St. Lawrence, since of Titley Court, County Hereford, baronet. Azure, semée of crosses crosslet, or; two batons in saltire, encircled with laurel branches, gold, between three plates. Crest: Or, the stem of a ship; or, a pigeon, wings endorsed, argent, in the beak a sprig of laurel, vert. Motto: "Extant recte factis proemia." These arms are limited in the grant to Sir Isaac Coffin and the descendants of his father, Nathaniel

2. Coffin, Pine, Portlege, County Devon, temp William I. The present representative of this most ancient family, as well as of the families Pine of East Downe and Pepys of Impington, is the Rev. John Pine-Coffin, of Portledge Azure, semée of crosses crosslet, or; three bezants quar-

tering the arms of Pine, Downe, Kelway, Ilcombe, Winslade, Birt, Hondesmore, Appleton, Gould, Penfound, and Pepys. Crests: First, a martlet, azure, charged on the breast with two bezants, a mullet for difference; second, a pine tree proper. Motto: "In tempestate floresco."

3 Coffin, Portland, County Dorset. Argent, a chevron between three mullets, pierced sable.

4. Coffin, Somersetshire. Gules, two bars embattled, or.

5. Coffin, Somersetshire Argent, three bezants and five crosses crosslet, or.

6 Coffyn. Azure, four bezants within five crosses crosslet, or; crest, a bird, or, between two cinque-foils, or, stalked and leaved, vert.

Sir Isaac's visit to Nantucket, 1826, when he founded his school there, was commemorated by a bronze medal he had struck off on the occasion, bearing an admirable effigy of Tristram in full length, and in the graceful garb of his period, on a base bearing the date 1642. The effigy is encircled with the inscription: "Tristram Coffin, the first of the race that settled in America;" on the obverse four hands in fraternal grasp surrounded with the injunction: "Do honor to his name—be united." At the same time he had printed and widely distributed among the descendants of Tristram a handsome broadside, relating in brief the principal incidents of his life and of his origin as then known.

The broadside presents the arms of Tristram, with the facsimile of his signature. Azure, four bezants within five crosses crosslet, or, crest, a bird, or, between two cinque-foils, argent, stalked and leaved, vert These are said to have been the arms of Sir William, who died in 1638, and whose monument still stands at Standon, in Essex, of which royal manor he was high steward. This is the sixth coat of arms of the Coffins described in the "General Armory," and may have been taken from "Weaver's Funeral Monuments," who gives the inscription, or from "The College of Arms."

The arms of Sir Isaac, granted in 1804, when created a baronet, also on the broadside, have already been stated, being the first described in the 'General Armory" of the name, as given above

In *The New England Historical and Genealogical Register* for October, 1881, reprinted separately, is an article entitled "The Name and Armorials of the Coffin Family," by Mr. John Coffin Jones Brown The article is replete with information upon his subject. The difference between the arms of North Devon, 1349 to 1699, and South seems simply the addition of a fourth bezant in chief Conjectures are not proof, but the suggestion is reasonable, that the fourth bezant, which is in the centre chief, may have been adopted to distinguish the Brixton branch from that of Portledge.

Before me are two mementos of the second centennial of the death of Tristram, in 1881—a plate and bowl, handsomely decorated in gold, with the coat of arms of the South Devonshire Coffins emblazoned on each, with the four bezants between the five crosses crosslet, or, with this motto. " Per tenebras speramus lumen de lumine." This is the motto of Hector Coffin—perhaps adopted by him in some moment of discouragement at finding his quest of the parentage of Tristram's grandfather, Nicholas, on a wrong scent. I may be equally unfortunate; but his efforts and mine, if not attended with success, may illumine the path through the darkness to the truth.

XIV.
TUCKETT'S VISITATIONS OF DEVON, PAGE 207.

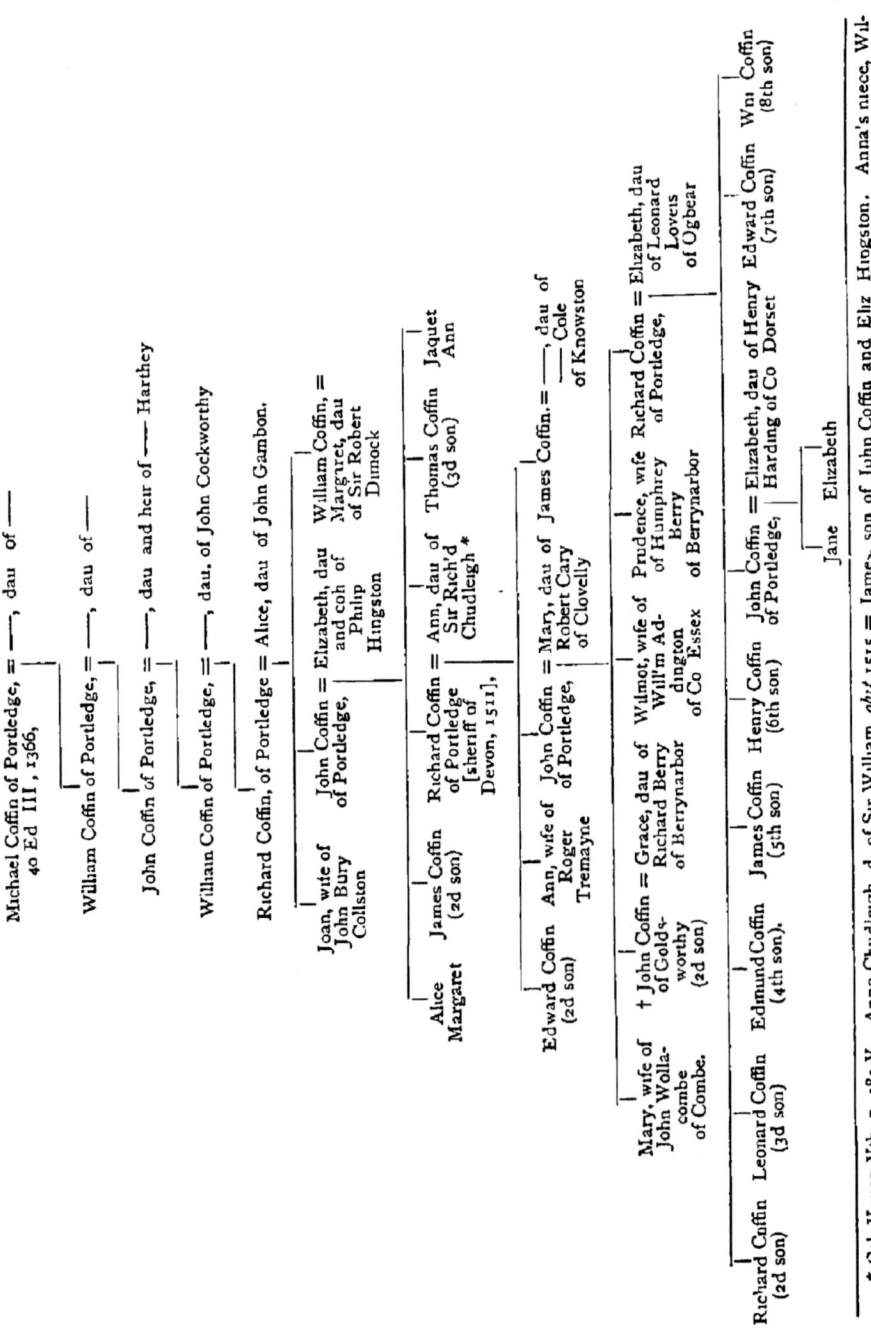

(Pedigree chart, read top-to-bottom along the stem:)

Michael Coffin of Portledge, = ———, dau of ———
40 Ed III, 1366,

William Coffin of Portledge, = ———, dau of ———

John Coffin of Portledge, = ———, dau and heir of —— Harthey

William Coffin of Portledge, = ———, dau. of John Cockworthy

Richard Coffin, of Portledge = Alice, dau of John Gambon.

Children of Richard Coffin and Alice:
- Joan, wife of John Bury Collston
- John Coffin of Portledge, = Elizabeth, dau and coh of Philip Hingston
- William Coffin, = Margret, dau of Sir Robert Dimock

Children of John Coffin and Elizabeth:
- Alice
- Margaret
- James Coffin (2d son)
- Richard Coffin of Portledge [sheriff of Devon, 1511], = Ann, dau of Sir Rich'd Chudleigh*
- Thomas Coffin (3d son)
- Jaquet
- Ann

Children of Richard Coffin and Ann:
- Edward Coffin (2d son)
- Ann, wife of Roger Tremayne
- John Coffin of Portledge, = Mary, dau of Robert Cary of Clovelly
- James Coffin = ———, dau of Cole of Knowston

Children of John Coffin and Mary:
- Mary, wife of John Wollacombe of Combe.
- Richard Coffin (2d son)
- Leonard Coffin (3d son)
- † John Coffin of Goldsworthy (2d son)
- Edmund Coffin (4th son)
- James Coffin (5th son)
- Wilmot, wife of Will'm Addington of Co Essex
- Henry Coffin (6th son) = Grace, dau of Richard Berry of Berrynarbor
- Prudence, wife of Humphrey Berry of Berrynarbor
- Richard Coffin of Portledge, = Elizabeth, dau of Leonard Loveis of Ogbear
- John Coffin = Elizabeth, dau of Henry Harding of Co Dorset
- Edward Coffin (7th son)
- W m Coffin (8th son)

Children of John Coffin and Elizabeth:
- Jane
- Elizabeth

Children of Henry Coffin and Grace:
- Humphrey Coffin, (aged 15)   Giles Coffin, (aged 10)   Nicholas Coffin, (aged 7)

* Col Vivian V:th, p. 189 V. Anna Chudleigh, d of Sir William *obit* 1515 = James, son of John Coffin and Eliz Hingston. Anna's niece, Wilmot, d of Sir Richard, *obit* 1558 = Richard Coffin, the sheriff of Devon, 1511   Two brothers = aunt and niece

† John Coffin of Goldsworthy (2d son), = Grace, dau of Richard Berry of Berrynarbor.

XV.

COFFIN DATES.

Richard, 1100, 1327, county records
Sir Hugo. of Combe Coffin, 1189-99.
Sir Geoffry, Henry III, 1216-72
    Sir William Pole, of 386 Portlage
Richard, 2 Knight fees of Robert the King's son.
Richard, 2 Knight fees of Henry Herring
Richard, 24 Edward I, 1296.
John, 8 Edward II, 1315.
David, 19 Edward III, 1346.
Michael, 40 Edward III, 1367.
William

John = Thomasia, d of Hathey.
William = d John Cockementon
Richard = Alice, d of John Sambon
{ William.
{ John = Elizabeth, co-d of Phillippa Hingeston.
{ James = Ann, d. of Sir Wm Chudleigh
{ Thomas.
{ Richard = Wilmot, d of Sir Richard Chudleigh.
William, son of above =
John = Mary, d of Rob. Cary, of Clovelly.
Richard.

OTHER MENTION OF COFFIN.

Richard, deed 1254, Henry III
William, lord of Alwenter, 1272, Edward I
Sir Richard, deed of Edward I
Richard = 1311.
{ John = 1318.
{ Roger.
{ Lawrence.
{ Richard
David = Thomasia, 32 Edward III, 1359.
David, son and heir of David, 1376

John and Thomasia, wife living, 1427
Richard, Sheriff of Devon, 2 Henry VIII, 1511
Richard, Sheriff of Devon, 36 Charles II, 1683.
{ John.
{ William = Margaret, d of Thomas Giffard
Eldest son.
John of Hyde in Northam
Richard = Honor, d Ed Prideaux of Padstow.
James, of Markleigh
Elizabeth, b 1566, d 1613 = Wyke of Som.

HEROLD'S VISITATION OF DEVON, 1620, P. 64.

Richard = Wilmot Chudleigh.
Edward
James = Mary Cole
John = Mary Cary.
{ Mary = John Wollacomb, 1589.
{ Prudence = Berrie of Berrie
{ Wilmot = William Addington = Farrington, 1590
{ John = Grace and Richard Berrie.
{ Humphrey, b. 1605, wasted his estate
{ Giles, b 1610.
{ Nicholas, b. 1613
{ Richard, 1589 = Elizabeth Loveis.

{ John = Elizabeth, d. Henry Harding
{ Jane.
{ Elizabeth
{ Richard
{ Leonard
{ Edward
{ James
{ Henry
{ Edward.
{ William
Seven daughters, Mary, Ibbot, Wilmot, Elizabeth, Christian, Julian, Katherine

CHURCH MONUMENTS.

John, 1572–1622
Richard, s of Richard, s. of John, 1659–60.
Richard, 1569–1622, age 48.
Elizabeth, his wife, 1571–1651, age 80
Ruth, 1601–42, age 41, wife of Hockin.

Richard, 1622–99
Bridget, widow of Kellond, 1676–97
John, 1678–1703
Ann, widow of Richard, 1655–1705.

BAPTISMS FROM PARISH REGISTER.

1569 Wilmot, d John
1573 Prudence.
1574 Richard.
1576 John
1592 Mary, d Richard.
1592 John, s. Richard
1603 Humphrey, s John
1605 ———, d John
1607 William, s. Richard, Esq
1608 Edward, s Richard, Esq
1618 Jane, d John

1619 Elizabeth, d John
1621 Gartred.
1654 Ruth, d Richard, Esq
1655 Elizabeth, d Richard, Esq
1657 Jane, d Richard, Esq
1658 Mary, d Richard, Esq
1659 Richard, s and 2, d Richard, Esq.
1660 Garthred, d Richard
1662 Ann, d Richard.
1664 Ann, d Richard

MARRIAGES FROM REGISTERS.

1589 Mr Richard Coffin and Eliz Lovers
1589 Mary, d, of John Wollacomb
1596 Wilmot, d John and Mary Cary = Farrington
1607 Mary, d. of Richard = Moore
1609 Ebbot = Levalles
1613 Margaret = Richard Pyne

1616 John, s and h of Richard = Harding
1617 Wilmot = Weekes
1623 Elizabeth = Fortescue.
1628 Elizabeth = Crust
1633 Katherine = Hocking

BURIALS FROM PARISH REGISTER.

1555 Richard, Esq
1569 Wilmot, widow
1571 John, s John
1591 William Addington.
1608 John, Esq
1617 Richard, Esq
1622 John, Esq.

1654 Elizabeth, d Richard.
1660 Richard, s and h of Richard, Esq.
1662 Ann, d Richard.
1663 James, gent
1665 Dorothy, wife of Richard.
1666 Elizabeth, d. of Richard.

XVI.

THE REFORMATION.

Sir William Coffin was born about 1480. The British realm was then all Catholic · bell, book, and candle, high mass, and confessionals, were paramount in chapel and church. Convents and other monastic institutions, with their cloistered walls and hidden ways, possessed a large portion of its most fertile soil its most picturesque territory. Religion, all the more sincere and honest for adversity, grew corrupt with a pampered priesthood, lost the respect and confidence of the laity. Their love of domination and arbitrary exactions created disaffection, and paved the way for a cross no longer a symbol. The indulgences sold by Leo the Tenth to build St. Peter's, glut his own extravagance and the greed of his favorites, aroused Christendom to a sense of the universal degeneracy that made a farce of faith.

If the motives of Henry the Eighth were not of the purest, the power of the throne and the good sense of the people co-operated to cast off a yoke become insupportable. England, insular and enlightened, took a leading part in the Reformation. From our present distant view, events must have moved rapidly to consummate so great a revolution in so brief a period. Conservative minds clung with tenacity to their old faith and institutions, and there was so much in the new repugnant and repulsive that it was only brought about amid great tribulation. Still, within thirty years England, in 1530 Catholic, became Protestant.

The presence at court of Sir William Coffin, the intimate relations between him and Henry for twenty years, shown in the bequest of his implements of the chase, of which they no doubt shared in the toils and pleasure often together, the position he held at the coronation of Ann Boleyn, give us reason to believe that his own theological opinions coincided with those of the King.

The bloated Bluebeard that occupies his niche in history differs so essentially in appearance and character from that kingly form and chivalric spirit, that intellectual expression and amiable disposition, that distinguished Henry when he mounted the throne, that some apology seems called for in taking any pride that Sir William Coffin was his friend. Coffin died in 1538, and the King had hardly entered upon that bloody career now regarded with execration In his earlier manhood few monarchs had been so much beloved and respected. But, thwarted in his reasonable hopes of domestic happiness by a marriage not of his own choosing, he became soured, arbitrary, self-indulgent. Still, the law of England, that kings can do no wrong, is apt to blind loyal subjects to nice distinctions, so far as respects them; and the favors conferred on Coffin by the King may have made him less disposed to criticise.

He had married Lady Mannors, of Derbyshire, for which county, in 1529, he was chosen Knight of the Shire to Parliament. While on his way to attend its sessions, passing by a churchyard, he observed near the road a multitude of people standing idle Inquiring the cause, he was told that they had brought a corpse thither to be buried, but the priest refused to do his office unless they delivered him the poor man's cow, the only quick goods he left, for a mortuary. Sir William sent for the priest, and required him to do his office to the dead, who peremptorily refused unless he had his mortuary first. Thereupon he ordered the priest to be put into the poor man's grave, and earth to be thrown in upon him; and, as he still persisted in his refusal, there was still more earth thrown in, until the obstinate priest was either altogether, or well-nigh, suffocated.

Now, thus to handle a priest in those days was a very audacious proceeding; but Sir William, with the favor he had at court and the interest he had in the House, diverted the storm. He so lively represented the mischievous consequences of priests' arbitrarily demanding mortuaries, that the then Parliament, taking it into their serious consideration, prohibited priests from exacting more than from three shillings to ten, according to the property left. This act against excessive mortuaries is classed by the historians, with two more, as bringing about the Reformation and England's declaration of independence of the Papal throne. It becomes of some importance as an historical event to be remembered. We mention it here as recalling similar incidents in the life of Tristram, when he took upon himself the sole responsibility of saving the wreckage at Nantucket; of Isaac, when he fought with the Brabanders against Austria or saved the burning ship by forcing the men back to their quarters.

XVII.

ALLEN COFFIN'S CALL OF TRISTRAM'S DESCENDANTS TO THE SECOND CENTENNIAL OF HIS DEATH IN 1881.

When I recently read the invitation of Mr Allen Coffin, in *The Inquirer*, of Nantucket, for December 6, 1879, to the then proposed gathering of the race at Nantucket to commemorate the death of Tristram, in 1681, it seemed so full of the information the readers of the present publication might need, that I wrote to request him to permit me to insert it wholly or in part. He generously consented In the faith that we have all but one motive—to bring within the reach of all of Tristram's descendants what sheds any additional light on his character and career—it is here presented. I find it difficult to omit any part of it, unless what in other forms has already found place.

A LEAF FROM THE LIFE OF MY GREAT-GRANDFATHER'S GREAT-GRANDFATHER

By Allen Coffin.

With the death of Edward the Confessor was practically terminated the Saxon dynasty of England. William, Duke of Normandy, whom Edward had appointed his successor, landed at Pevensey, on the 28th of September, 1066. He met Harold on the field near Hastings, and, after a long battle, Harold fell pierced with an arrow, and his soldiers fled from the field panic-stricken. The Norman conquest was thus achieved, and William the Conqueror soon after crowned king

Accompanying William was an army of sixty thousand men, volunteers from adjacent parts of the continent, who crowded to his camp at the mouth of the Dive, eager to share in the vicissitudes of the campaign. This was a wonderfully romantic age, and William was aided by many sovereigns and princes, and a vast body of nobility from the different kingdoms. Those who accompanied the Conqueror became the barons, and knights, and esquires, and sergeants of feudal times, and in the divisions of the riches of the conquered domain became proprietors of vast estates, castles, abbeys, villages, and even whole towns.

There was one man among William's conquering host in whom most of this large assembly will ever have an abiding interest. He was a general of the army, and his name was Richard Coffyn. From what province he came, or what ancestry he boasted, or what life he had pursued prior to his adventurous campaign, are facts which no friendly hand has yet lifted from the shrouds of oblivion. He shared in the spoils of the conquest, became a tenant of the crown, and his name was written in the Domesday Book. All of the followers of William were noble in right of their victory and foreign birth, and the parish of Alwington, in the county of Devon, appears to have been conferred upon him, with the title of Sir Richard Coffin, Knight, etc. Portledge was the Coffin manor, and, through a period of more than eight centuries, streaming down to the present time, an unbroken line of inheritance has been preserved.

In the history of the County of Devon, in England, honorable mention is made of Sir Ellis Coffin, Knight of Clist and Ingarby, in the days of King John, of Sir Richard Coffin, of Alwington, in the time of Henry II.; of Sir Jeffrey Coffin and Combe Coffin under Henry III, and numerous other knightly descendants during successive reigns, till the time of Henry VIII. Sir William Coffin, Sheriff of Devonshire, was highly preferred at the court of Henry VIII, and accompanied the king as one of the eighteen chosen by him on a tournament in France in 1519. He was Master of the Horse at the coronation of Anne Boleyn, and a gentleman of the Privy Council. He was also High Steward of the Manor and Liberties of Standon, County of Hertford At his death he bequeathed to his royal master, King Henry, with whom he had been in especial grace and favor, all of his hawks, and his best horses and cart. As he left no issue, he conveyed the Manor of East Higginston, County of Devon, to his eldest brother's son, Richard Coffin, Esq, of Portledge. Sir William's monument, in Standon Church, is mentioned in "Weever's Funeral Monuments" (p. 534).

Nicholas Coffin, of Brixton (one account says Butler's Parish), in Devonshire, in his will, dated September 12, 1613, and proved November 3, 1613, mentions his wife Joan and sons Peter, Nicholas, Tristram, John, and daughter Anne. He was the grandfather to the emigrant to New England.

Peter Coffin, of Brixton, in his will, dated December 1, 1627, and proved March 13, 1628, provided that his wife, Joan Thember, shall have possession of the land during her life, and then the said property shall go to his son and heir, Tristram, "who is to be provided for according to his degree and calling." His son John is to have certain property when he becomes twenty years of age. He mentions his daughters Joan, Deborah, Eunice, and Mary, and refers to his tenement in Butler's Parish called Silferhay. He was the father of the emigrant

John Coffin, of Brixton, an uncle of the emigrant, who died without issue, in his will, dated January 4, 1628, and proved April 3, 1628, appoints his nephew, Tristram Coffin, his executor, and gives legacies to all of Tristram's sisters, all under twelve years of age.

I have been led to seek the cause of Tristram's removal to America, but upon that subject the oracles are silent and tongues dumb. Was it that he might enjoy a larger religious liberty, or to escape persecution, or was it the same love of adventure that induced his ancestor, Sir Richard Coffin, to embark with the Duke of Normandy six centuries before? Let us look at the contemporaneous history of England. We shall find that the time which covers Tristram's mature life in England, about fifteen years, marks a most eventful period—the moment when intellectual freedom was claimed unconditionally by Englishmen as an inalienable right, and when ecclesiastical forms were not spared by the revolution of the times.

James I., whose reign had been adorned by Shakespeare and Bacon, died in 1625, when Tristram was twenty years old. Charles I. had been upon the throne but two years when Tristram's father died. The Petition of Right, in 1628, sought to limit the powers of the Crown, and the King soon after abolished the Parliament and established the Star Chamber. Puritanism was making rapid strides, and large numbers of Puritans were leaving England. So great was the exodus that the King prohibited their departure, and Hampden, Pym, and Cromwell were prevented from leaving. About this time the Duke of Buckingham was assassinated. In 1638 the Scots, to maintain their ecclesiastical rights, took up arms against the King, having formed the celebrated Solemn League and Covenant, and sustained the Parliament in its opposition to Charles. The Earl of Strafford and Archbishop of Canterbury, as chief advisers of the King, were impeached and beheaded (the former in 1641, and the latter in 1644). The Presbyterians, who were now a majority in the Commons, procured the exclusion of Bishops from the House of Lords, in 1641, which was followed by an act in 1643 entirely abolishing Episcopacy, so Charles began to realize that without Bishops there would be no King. Under these circumstances the Lord Parliament convened

The irrepressible conflict between Charles and the Parliament came to a crisis in 1642, and in August of that year the royal standard was raised at Nottingham. The King was generally supported by the nobility, the landed gentry, the High Church party, and the Catholics; and the Parliament was sustained by the mercantile and middle classes, and the lower order of the great towns. On which side of this conflict would Tristram Coffin most naturally have gone? He was of the landed gentry, and, I think, a High Churchman. Conformably to his father's will, he was to be provided for "according to his degree and calling." He must therefore have had a calling—a profession—he may have taken holy orders. He was unquestionably a royalist and a Cavalier, and the very year of the appeal to arms, 1642, after the conflict had been waged, Tristram Coffin, at the age of thirty-seven, left all of his comfortable estates in Old England and embarked for America, bringing with him his wife and five small children, his mother, then aged fifty-eight, and two unmarried sisters, and none of them ever returned. I believe that, having embraced the royal cause, he was compelled to leave England, and took with him all of his near relatives; that his valuable estates at Dorsetshire and at Brixton, the tenements in Butler's Parish, mentioned in his father's and uncle's wills, were sequestrated. That he was a leading spirit in the time of Charles I., and proved his loyalty by unmistakable acts which rendered him obnoxious to the Roundheads and Parliament fanatics, I have unshaken confidence.

He was rich in England—he was otherwise when landed in America. He married Dionis Stevens, of Brixton, County of Devon. He first settled at Salisbury, Mass., and the same year removed to Haverhill, where his name appears as a witness to an Indian deed of that place, dated November 15, 1642. Three more children were born to them in Haverhill, and one at Newbury. Of their nine children, the last born in England and the first born in America died in infancy. All of the others married and had children. He was licensed to keep an inn at Newbury, and a ferry across the Merrimac River. He subsequently returned to Salisbury and became a county magistrate.

He came to Nantucket in 1659 on a prospecting voyage, having obtained Peter Folger from Martha's Vineyard as an interpreter of the Indian language. The company which purchased the island was formed at Salisbury after his return. His son, James Coffin, who came in the boat with the family of Thomas Macy, which voyage Whittier has immortalized in his poem of "The Exiles," had doubtless accompanied his father on the former voyage. All of the early deeds conveying land in Nantucket to this company recite first the name of Tristram Coffin as a grantee. He and his sons at one time owned about one-fourth part of Nantucket, and the whole of Tuckernuck.

I do not think that personal religious persecutions had anything to do with his removal to Nantucket, although he doubtless despised the intolerant spirit of Essex County, which prompted the flights of Roger Williams and Thomas Macy, notwithstanding he was at the time a county magistrate.

His place of residence in Nantucket is described in a deed as being at Northam or Coppomet Harbor (Capaum Pond being probably open to the sea), near the old shear-pen gate. He doubtless had other houses in this vicinity, where a village grew up around him, and a monument has recently been placed upon the spot supposed to have been his homestead.

He was the first Chief Magistrate of the island, having been commissioned by Lord Lovelace, on the 29th of June, 1671; and, together with Thomas Mayhew, who was the first Chief Magistrate of Martha's Vineyard, and two associates from each island, constituting a General Court for the two islands, enacted the first prohibitory liquor law of which the world has any record—a marvel of legal preciseness and acumen.

He died in Nantucket, on the third day of October, A D. 1681, at the age of seventy-six, and probably sleeps in the ancient burial-ground on the hill, just east of Maxcy's Pond.

> "The earliest ray of the golden day
> On that hallowed spot is cast;
> And the evening sun as he leaves the world
> Looks kindly on that spot last"

One year from next October will occur the second centenary of the death of Tristram Coffin. The multitude of descendants all over the world who claim him with pride as their common ancestor may desire to rear a suitable monument to his memory in the land where he died, and where his liberal, high-minded, and Christian character, not inappropriately compared by Benjamin Franklin Folger with that of William Penn, found such practical opportunity of expression in his relations with the Indians I feel that I echo the sentiments of the descendants in Nantucket when I invite all the other descendants to a grand reunion of the Coffin family in Nantucket, in October, 1881, to participate in exercises commemorative of a noble life—the life of our common ancestor, Tristram Coffin, the first of his name in America.

PREPARATIONS IN 1881.

THE CLAN —The Coffin Reunion is now so near at hand that we are enabled to make some statements of fact concerning the same. The New

Bedford brass Band will arrive on the morning of the 16th, in time to proceed to Surf-side where the clam-bake is to be provided. The clam-bake about noon will be gotten up by A. F. Copeland, of Boston, and will include chowders, baked and fried fish of the different varieties, lobsters, etc., garnished with the products of the season.

The oration on this occasion will be by Tristram Coffin, Esq, of Poughkeepsie, N. Y., a gentleman well qualified by name and attainments to do ample justice to the occasion. An original poem will be read, and other literary exercises will follow, interspersed with music.

On the second day, Wednesday, the seventeenth of August, the memorial exercises will be held at the Atheneum Hall, on which occasion Charles Carleton Coffin, of Boston, will make the oration, and a poem by Robert Barry Coffin, Esq, of New York, will be read. Other speeches will be introduced on this occasion, as may be hereafter arranged. These exercises will take place in the forenoon, and in the afternoon a pilgrimage will be made to the old homestead place of Tristram Coffin near Capaum Pond, accompanied with the Band of Music, where appropriate commemorative exercises will be held. It is proposed to have some entertainment in the evening at the Atheneum Hall, the precise character of which has not been fully decided upon.

The last day's exercises will consist of a Breakfast or Banquet at Surf-side, at which Mr. Copeland will make his best endeavor to lay tables in the highest style of his profession. The Committee make assurances that this affair will surpass any previous effort of the kind ever made upon the island. The dessert will be served in plates of the finest French china, decorated with the Coffin Coat of Arms, and the coffee and tea in a new style cup and saucer decorated with the same arms, and imported expressly for this occasion by Charles E. Wiggin, of Boston. Prof Selden J. Coffin, of Lafayette College, Easton, Pa., will make the oration after this repast, and Dr. Arthur Elwell Jenks, of Nantucket, will read an original poem. Other literary and musical exercises will follow, and the afternoon's exercises will conclude with an anthem written for the occasion, in which the entire family will be invited to join, the accompaniment being performed by the Band.

In the evening, at Surf-side, a Grand Ball will impart a festive concluding feature of the Reunion exercises, Smith's Quadrille Band furnishing the music. This, like all the other exercises, is expected to be the most *recherché* affair ever indulged in upon the island.

MESSRS. EDITORS—Rumors of the Coffin gathering have been in the air even here for some time, and lately the *Inquirer and Mirror*, with the names of its publishers, familiar a quarter of a century ago, has come to us, bringing a more definite word. Although over twenty years have passed since I could claim to be a citizen of your island, interest in Nantucket, especially the Nantucket of thirty or forty years ago, has suffered no diminution. Most people have but *one* home, and let them go where they may, in the fairest of lands even, in their hours of quiet reflection, and especially when the shadows of their life begin to lengthen, the sun seems to shine with greater brightness on the spot where they passed their childhood. So it is with our home on the "Isle of the Sea." And these rumors of the Coffin gathering have revived the old associations, and peopled your homes and streets with those who once filled them. Every spot, from Siasconset to Maddaket, and down to the South Shore, has been gone over, and anecdote, tradition, and legend have come up, perhaps to be told to some little company who were not so *favored* as to be born on the island, but who never tire of hearing about it.

By the way, your humble correspondent was asked a year or two ago to contribute one of a course of lectures given here for some local charity. Having often spoken to the larger part of the probable audience, and being too much occupied to write anything new, I tried to beg off. "Can't you just talk about Nantucket, as you have done in company?" "Why, the people here don't care about that." "But you *must* do something." "Well, if you will take the responsibility, I will give such a talk." And so I did. Just brushed up my history, you know, especially of Revolutionary times, telling the people that no town contributed more, negatively, by its losses and sufferings, to the cause of National freedom than Nantucket. Then I talked about the whale-fishery and sea life. You see if I made mistakes there, or *embellished a little where it was necesssary*, no one of my audience of lands-people knew it. Then I told about "sheep-shearing," and the good old Society of Friends, the mother church, and a good one as we could find before the seeds of strife came in and quenched the simple charities of the beautiful island life. Then I drew portraits, and told anecdotes of the notables, Keziah Coffin and her country house; Cousin Elizabeth Black, with her wondrous speech, Franklin Folger, and others, ending with a quotation from Whittier's sweet ballad, "The Exiles," so dear to a Nantucketer. The audience paid the tribute (not to the speaker, but to the island and its people) of profound attention, with mingled seriousness and laughter, for an hour, and the expression is still occasionally given that the evening on Nantucket was one of most enjoyable interest.

Thus it is everywhere. There seems to have been something in the original stock, or the environments, in the business, the social and religious atmosphere, or the pure sea breezes of the island, which made it a place that every wanderer soon learns to be proud of; and that you who are left to sustain the honors of the old town may well think of with satisfaction. How well and nobly the town's decline was striven against, especially after the great fire. Is it not recorded in some book of light, to the credit of many, both of those who have passed on and you who are left? And it almost seemed, when I read of the inauguration of the railroad, that your crowning had come. I confess to a latent wish not to have the old-time customs too much lost in the modernisms of a fashionable watering-place. We can get these somewhere else; at Nantucket we want Nantucket. To go to the South Shore in a cart-bodied wagon somehow seems most natural. But that perhaps is sentiment only, and people can't live on sentiment; so I am glad to learn of improvement, and hope that you all who have nobly striven for it and tried to keep things up will reap a reward. Whether a closely occupied life will allow me to be at your gathering is yet uncertain. I shall try for it, anyway. I wanted to make sure, through your columns, if you will allow it to an old friend of expressing interest in the reunion; and will you pardon a suggestion, which may be superfluous. At the centennial celebrations at Concord and Lexington, I noticed that those less familiar with the spots of interest than we who live near, found great satisfaction in looking at the placards which marked historic places and houses. To the Coffin family especially there are many such places at Nantucket. Mary Starbuck, the "great woman," daughter of Tristram Coffin, and wife of Nathaniel Starbuck, will be thought of with much interest. Where her house stood is generally known. It may not be so well known that the house, moved down, is still standing and retaining much of its original form. The house of William Rotch, Sr, is also standing, moved up from lower Main street, and in shape is unchanged. I have the authority of Franklin Folger for these statements If you care to identify these places, and some others, and some islander cannot readily do it for you, I shall be happy to write to you further. Won't you want to designate the spot "up west," which was the birthplace of Dr. Franklin's mother, and the first Friends' burying-ground, where Mary Starbuck was buried, and the house in town where Lucretia Mott was born, and lived until she was twelve years old, and the site of Keziah (Miriam) Coffin's house, where, in the Revolution, she sold smuggled goods to the distressed islanders; and the site of the old Friends' meeting-house, corner of Main and Pleasant Streets—an unsightly structure, guiltless of paint or architectural design, but to many of us a sacred spot in memory, especially at "quarterly meeting time," when the immense building was crowded in every part with hushed and reverent worshippers, and the sweet tones of some gifted messenger of the gospel (perhaps Elizabeth Robinson, from England) breathed around the old oaken braces and timbers, holding us children in reverent awe? Shall we ever hear the like again? No; but something else, and in some respects something better, has come to take its place Won't you want to write large the old doggerel we used to repeat, even if it does depreciate the Husseys, one line of which is,

" The Coffins, noisy, fractious, loud,"

not omitting the last stanza, of which I only heard within the year, that ends,

" The Pinkhams beat the devil."

How they beat him, my esteemed friend B., who sent me the stanza, did not inform me. And so we might go on, from North Shore to Newtown. If I can do anything to promote the interest or enjoyment of your reunion it will give me great pleasure.

In meeting here and there with ex-Nantucketers who are interested in the island, even if they give less sign of interest than some others, it has seemed to us that there is a dearth of circulars or something to tell us what to do. If it be not much, it will have the merit of a hearty regard for old and new Nantucket. Do save us a copy of the albertype of Tristram Coffin's house, at Newbury. A friend of ours this way has a friend who has been in the house in old England from which the Coffin's came. It is now about eight hundred years old, and is still occupied and well preserved. This lady, who is herself a descendant of the Coffins, has a view of the house, which I hope to see. Can't you get copies for your gathering? Hoping with some of my family to ride over the railroad, and in a "cart-bodied wagon," too, next month, and to take the hands of many whom I used to meet in other days, and still hold *in much esteem*, I am

Yours,
C. C. HUSSEY.

BILLERICA, July 28, 1881

[We are pleased to hear from our former schoolfellow of over half a century ago, whom we had supposed had long since been gathered to his fathers. Although we were one of the small boys, and he one of the big ones at the opening of the Coffin School in 1827, we well remember him as the acknowledged leader of the "Chookies" in our snow-ball battles with the "Newtowners," which were carried on with such relentless fury in those times. We would inform him that there are still quite a number of the "Clio boys" living, and suppose many of them would be willing to open a correspondence with him. Benjamin F. Coffin and Franklin Folger still reside on Nantucket; Robert G. Coffin in San Francisco; David P Eldridge in Milford, Mass.; Frederick A. Hussey in Brookline, Mass, and Andrew J Morton in Boston. The rest of the boys are dead, only two of whom died at home, one from sickness, and one—Edward Worth—drowned at Brant Point.—EDS.]

When the time arrived for the celebration, hundreds of the descendants of Tristram flocked to Nantucket from all over the continent. They were cordially greeted and warmly welcomed by their kindred belonging to the Island. The weather did not prove altogether propitious. The winds blew cold and the rain fell in torrents. Occasional intervals of sunshine gave hope of permanent clearing, but several of the promised repetitions of the festal ways of the earliest times were given up. Enough, however, of the pleasures prepared remained practicable, to render the event one long to be remembered.

XVIII.

WILLS.

WILL OF SIR ISAAC COFFIN.

(*Extracted from the Principal Registry of the Probate, Divorce, and Admiralty Division of the High Court of Justice, in the Prerogative Court of Canterbury.*)

THIS is my last Will and Testament, hereby revoking all others I may have heretofore made. Having disposed of all my property in England that I had in the funds to my nearest relations, named in a Deed of Trust, I bequeath the Magdalen Islands, in the Gulf of St Lawrence, to my nephew, John Townsend Coffin, during the term of his natural life, then, at his demise, to his son Isaac Tristram Coffin, and his issue male. Should the said Isaac Tristram Coffin leave no issue male, then to his brothers in succession and their male heirs; failing in male heirs in that family I then leave the said Magdalen Islands to my nephew Henry Edward Coffin and his male issue; he failing to have issue male I then bequeath the said islands to the sons of my late Cousin, William Coffin, in succession, and their male heirs; failing in male heirs of said William Coffin, then the islands to become the property of the sons of my Cousin Thomas Coffin, of Three Rivers, Lower Canada, in succession; should they die and leave no issue male, I then give the said Magdalen Islands to my Godson Isaac Campbell Coffin, now an officer in the East India Company's Service, and his sons in succession; failing in issue male from the said Isaac Coffin, I give the said Islands to his brother Sebright Coffin; should all these above enumerated Coffins die without issue male, then I leave the said Islands to my nephew, Commander William Barwell and his issue male; failing to have male heirs, I then leave the said Magdalen Islands to the person who may prove to be my Heir-at-Law As the Islands were granted to me for my services during the American War, 1775–1783, and in Canada during Lord Dorchester's time, I request they may remain as an Heir-Loom in the family, and that whoever succeeds to them may assume and bear the Arms of Coffin. My property at Boston, N. America, under the care of

William Foster Otis, Esq., amounting by the last account to Eleven thousand five hundred pounds, I desire may be left under his control until it amounts to Twenty Thousand pounds, then the interest to be paid to John Townsend Coffin and the principal to Isaac Tristram Coffin, he having no children, then to his brothers in succession, on the demise of the Father John Townsend Coffin; failing in male issue, the Family of the said John Townsend Coffin. Then the Twenty thousand pounds to be divided among any female children the said John Townsend Coffin may leave. I name Charles Earle, Esq, William Earle, Esq, Hardman Earle, Esq., Richard Earle, Esq, Barrister, and William Foster Otis, Esq., of the City of Boston, N. America, as my Trustees and Executors, requesting as an old friend of their families they will forgive the trouble I give them.

           ISAAC COFFIN, Admiral. [L.S.]

Signed, sealed, and delivered in the presence
 of us, the 15th day of March, 1839.
    JNO. S. CARDEN, Real Adm'l, Cheltenham.
    S. MARTIN COLQUITT, R. N., Do. Cheltenham

 This is a Codicil to my Will. Unable to make a distribution of my property among my relations, from the difficulty attending my obtaining a release from the Trustees of the late Lady Coffin, I hereby leave to my Trustees, named in my Will, with all my funded property in the Three pr. Cent Consols and reduced annuities, the interest, amounting to Seven hundred and thirty-eight pounds, to be paid to my nephew, John Townsend Coffin, at his death, the said interest to be paid to Isaac Tristram Coffin and his heirs lawfully begotten.

           ISAAC COFFIN, Admiral.

[L.S.]

  Signed, sealed, and delivered in the presence
   of us, the subscribing trustees.
    THOMAS ROE, Major H. E. I. Cs. S.,
    GEORGE DIXON, Vicar of Helmsley, Yorkshire.

 Appeared personally, Samuel Martin Colquitt, of the Parish of Cheltenham, in the County of Gloucester, Esquire, made oath that he is one of the subscribed witnesses to the last Will and Testament of Sir Isaac Coffin, late of Cheltenham, in the County of Gloucester, Baronet, deceased, who died on the twenty-third day of July last, the said will bearing date the fifteenth day of March, one thousand eight hundred and thirty nine. And he further made oath that he was present at the execution of the said Will by the said deceased, and that the said Will was signed at the foot or the end thereof in manner, as now appears by the said Testator, in the presence of this deponent and of John Surram Carden, the other witness thereto subscribed, present at the same time, who set and subscribed their names as witnesses to the said will in the presence of the said Testator.   S. MARTIN COLQUITT, R N.

On the 24th day of December, 1839, the said Samuel Martin Colquitt, Esquire, was duly sworn to the truth of the above Affidavit before me,
FRANCIS CLOSE,
Perpetual Curate of Cheltenham, Commissioner.

Appeared personally Thomas Roe, of Cheltenham, in the County of Gloucester, Esquire, and made oath that he is one of the subscribed witnesses to the Codicil to the last will and Testament of Sir Isaac Coffin, late of Cheltenham, in the County of Gloucester, Baronet, deceased, who died on the twenty-third day of July last, the said Will bearing date the Fifteenth day of March, one thousand eight hundred and thirty nine, and the said Codicil being without date. And he further made oath that he was present at the execution of the said Codicil by the said deceased, on or about the Fifteenth or Twentieth day of May last, and he further made oath that the said Codicil was signed at the end or foot thereof in manner as now appears by the said Testator in the presence of this deponent and of the Reverend George Dixon, Clerk, the other subscribed witness thereto, both present at the same time, who set and subscribed their names as witnesses to the said Codicil in the presence of the said Testator.   THOMAS ROE.

On the thirteenth day of January, 1840, the said Thomas Roe, Esq., was duly sworn to the truth of the aforesaid Affidavit before me,
FRANCIS CLOSE,
Perpetual Curate of Cheltenham, Gloucestershire, Commrs.

Proved at London (with a Codicil), 15 January, 1840, before the Judge by the oath of William Earle, Esq, one of the Executors to whom admon was granted, having been first sworn by Commissioner, duly to administer. Power reserved of making the like grant to Charles Earle, Hardman Earle, and Richard Earle, Esquires, and William Foster Otis, the other Executors when they shall apply for the same. Effects under £25,000.

The descendants of William Gayer and of his admirable daughters, Damaris and Dorcas, are so many and so estimable that in the faith that they may be pleased to possess the wills of William and his brother Sir John, they are printed here from the "New England Gen. Register, vol. xxxi, p. 297. Mr. Folger furnished full copies of these Wills, to be preserved in the archives of the N. E. Historic Genealogical Society.

WILL OF WILLIAM GAYER, SR., ESQ.

I, William Gayer, of the Island of Nantucket, being sick but of sound mind and memory, make this my last will. Unto my son William Gayer, one Share of land on the Island of Nantucket, with all the privileges belonging (if my said son shall ever come hither again). To my dau. Damaris Coffin, one eighth part of a share of land on the Island of Nantucket, of that land I had of my Father-in-law, Edward Starbuck. I give my daughter, Dorcas Starbuck, one Eighth part of a Share of [said] land. My part of the Island of Muskeget to my two daughters, Damaris Coffin and Dorcas Starbuck, Equally to be divided between them. To my house-keeper, Patience Foot, one Cow and forty Sheep with Commonage for them as also half of the barn and try house, with half the garden, half the land and fence, about my dwelling house, half the lot and fence towards Monomoy, the horse pasture Exepted, as also the West Chamber and Garret, and half the lean to of my now dwelling house I give to Africa, a negro, once my servant, twenty Sheep and Commonage for them and for one horse, as also the East Chamber of my now dwelling house, and half the leanto, and the other half of my barn and try house with the half of all the lands and fence about my house, and the half of the lot towards Monomoy. I will that my dau., Damaris Coffin, have the use of the rest of my Dwelling house, if she should come hither to live. My two Daughters, Damaris Coffin and Dorcas Starbuck, Joynt Executrices of this my last will and testament.

WILLIAM GAYER

Sept. 21, 1710.

In presence of
RICHARD GARDNER, ELEAZER FOLGER, JUNR., EUNICE GARDNER, JABEZ BUNKER, JUDITH GARDNER.

Probated 24 day Oct. 1710.
ELEAZER FOLGER, Regr.

JAMES COFFIN,
Judge of Probate.

Sir John Gayer's Will.

I John Gayer, of Bombay, Knight, in perfect health do make this my last Will and Testament. My Body to be Interred at the Discretion of my hereafter named Executrix, and if I die in India, in the tomb of my former Wife Debts discharged I give as followeth: Unto my Brother William Gayer, of the Island of Nantucket, One Hundred Pounds Sterling. Unto his son, William Gayer, my nephew, now in the East Indies, Eight Thousand Pounds Sterling. Unto the children of Eldest Sister Jane Lee, Five Hundreds Pound Sterling, to be Equally devided amongst them, and in case of any of their Mortality, before Marriage, their part to the Survivor. Unto the children of my Sister, Joan Hooper, Seven Hundred Pounds Sterling, to be Equally Divided amongst them, and in Case of Either of their Mortality before Marriage their part to the Survivor. Unto the children of my Sister, Elizabeth Matthews, Two Hundred Pounds Sterling, to be Equally Devided amongst them, etc. Unto my Niece Elizabeth Gayer, Two Thousand Pounds Sterling to be kept in the hands of my Execturix and Improved by her for her maintenance while she lives a single life; but if she Marry, at the Day of her Marriage, the Principal and what is gained thereby, except so much as Defrays the Charge of her Maintenance before, is all to be paid her, but in Case of her Decease before Marriage, then that sum of Two Thousand Pounds, with what is Gained thereby I give to my Above Mentioned Nephew, William Gayer, to be forthwith paid him, besides the sum of Eight Thousand Pounds before Mentioned. Unto the children of Robert Harper, my Deceased wife's Brother, Three Hundred Pounds Sterling, to be Equally devided amongst them etc. Unto Joseph Harper, my Deceased wife's Brother, if he be alive at the time of my Decease, One Hundred Pounds Sterling. Unto the children of my Cousin, Mercy Throgmorton, Four Hundred Pounds Sterling etc. Unto the children of my Cousin John Rither, deceased, Two Thousand Pounds Sterling etc Unto my cousin, James Car, Two Hundred Pounds Sterling, in case he survives me. Unto my Cousin, Elizabeth Thrip, Ten Pounds Sterling Unto the children of Sister-in-Law, Judith Battin, Two Hundred Pounds Sterling, to be Equally devided Amongst them etc. Unto my Cousin, Lucy hole, fifty Pounds Sterling. Unto my Cousin, Rachel Dale, if she be alive at the time of my Decease, Ten Pounds Sterling. Unto my loving Friend, Mr. Thomas Wooley, Secretary of the East India Company, Fifty Pounds Sterling. Unto my loving Friend, Mr. Barnard Wiche, of Surrat, Fifty Pounds Sterling. Unto Mr. Robert Luynfer, of Surrat, Fifty Pounds Sterling, if he be alive at the time of my Decease. I Dedicate and Devote to God, for the Service of his Church, Five Thousand Pounds Sterling, to be disposed of by the persons hereafter mentioned, to yonng Students for the Ministry and to such as are Newly Entered into the Sacred Office, to furnish them with What [may be] Needful to make them most useful in the discharge of that great trust for which they are devoted to God; and it's my Earnest desire that those persons amongst whom this sum shall be distributed, may be men of Sober, Moderate principles, not inclined to Domination, nor to unnecessary Seperation, and to Express my mind more fully, I say unto men of such Principles as the late Reverend and truly Worthy Mr. Richard Baxter was, in whom the Primitive Spirit of holiness, Love, and Moderation did brightly shine, from whose works I give God thanks I have received great benefit. Now, the persons I most earnestly request in Conjunction with my wife and Nephew William Gayer to undertake the Distributing of I have so solemnly devoted, are the Right Worshipfull Henry Ashurst, Bant, and Mr. Thomas Wooley, before mentioned I do further request that they will all be assisting to my Beloved Wife in the whole management of her affairs.

If my Estate amounts to less than what is in my present books, Ending the last of July, 1710, when it arrives in England, amounting what is in Rupees at two shillings and six pence to a Rupee, then I order that Every Legacy herein mentioned shall be so much less in proportion as the whole of my Estate at the time of all its arrival in England falls Short of what it is in Said books. The rest of my Estate, whether Money, Plate, Gold or Silver, Jewels, Goods, Household Furniture, wearing Apparel, Books, Debts, Lands, and whatsoever, both Real and Personal, I shall be possessed of at my decease, I give unto my wife, Dame Mary Gayer, whom I make Sole Executrix of this, my last will and Testament. In witness Whereof I have hereunto set my hand and Seal in Bombay Castle, 5th of October, 1710   JOHN GAYER.

In presence of us, where no stampt paper is procurable, &c., &c., &c.,
WILLIAM AISLABIE, WILLIAM BARNES, ABRAHAM BARNOT, RICHARD WILMER, JOHN HILL.

A true copy from the original.
Witnesses, JOHN EATON DODSWORTH, JAMES OSBORNE, WILLIAM GAYER, RICHARD BULL.

WILL OF WILLIAM GAYER, JUNR.

9th Nov., 1712.

I, William Gayer, Gentleman of yᵉ Parish of Beckenham in Kent, being sick, but of sound and disposing mind and memory, do make my last will. Payment of all debts To my elder sister, Damaris Coffin, one-half part. To my younger sister, Dorcas Starbuck, yᵉ other half of what belongs to me in New England. To my two sisters aforesaid, two thousand pounds sterling, that is, to each one thousand pounds. To my aunt, Jane Lee, of Plymouth, Aunt Elizabeth Matthews, Mr Epiphamius Holland [each] £100 To Mr. George Musole, £25. To Mrs Martha Deacon, Mrs Abigail Fitch [each] £100 Remainder of my estate to my wife, Elizabeth Gayer, whom I appoint sole Executrix of this my last Will. WILLIAM GAYER.

In yᵉ presence of
SUSANNA HOLLAND, WILLIAM NORMAN, ANDREW STODDART.

XIX.

CORRESPONDENCE.

WILLIAM GAYER, Esq , came to this country from Devonshire, England.* He married Dorcas Starbuck, daughter of Elder Edward Starbuck, by his wife, Katherine Reynolds, of Wales. He was an early settler of Nantucket , probably had been a ship-carpenter ; was a farmer and a Justice of the Peace. I find by the records in the office of our Secretary of State, that Captain John Gardner and Mr. William Gayer were representatives to the General Court from Nantucket on the 8th of June, 1692, being the first representatives from that island after its transfer from the Colony of New York to the Province of Massachusetts Bay. William Gayer, Esq , was one of five judges appointed by the Governor of Massachusetts, in 1704, to try an Indian of Nantucket, named Sabo, for the crime of murder.

He lived in a double house, one and a half stories in height, on Church Street, in Nantucket, occupied long since my first remembrance by descendants of his daughter, Damaris Coffin. This house for a long time was considered the oldest on the island, and I think was built in 1682, of solid oak timber, the growth of the island, and strengthened with oak knees, like a ship, and very firmly. It passed into the hands of strangers about 1839 or 1840, and was taken down to give place to a modern dwelling-house. A bureau with a sort of book-case or cupboard on top—which was made in Oliver Cromwell's time, and brought over by William Gayer, probably in Charles the Second's reign, belonged to my grandmother, a great-granddaughter of William Gayer, Esq. It was made in part of English oak, colored a dark red, and ornamented with turned pieces of maple, painted black and nailed on ; and the top part, or cupboard, was in part supported by two maple urns, or short pillars, painted black It was altogether an unique but useful piece of furniture After the death of both of my grandparents, it was placed in the cabinet of curiosities of the Nantucket Atheneum, but was burned up in the great fire of 1846, when that building, with

---

* N. E Gen. and Hist Register, vol xxxi , page 297.

its fine collections of books, South Sea shells, war weapons, etc., was destroyed

The following letter is from Jane Gayer, mother of William Gayer, Sr., from Plymouth, England, to her son, William Gayer, at Nantucket:

"Son, my dearest love to you and your wife, and to my grandchildren, hoping that these few lines will find you in good health, as through mercy I enjoy at this present writing. I have sent you two letters by Mr. Blag, of New York, and I have sent several letters by other means, but I never received none from you since the 1st of October, 1692, bearing this date. Dear son, I should request you that I might hear from you. Your brother Sir John sailed from the downs the last of May, was a 12 month gone, and all his family with him. A month after he went away he put in for the Madeira. I received a letter from him out of the Madeira's, since I have not heard from him, for there has not a ship come home from that place since. I did not know whether there was a New England man here or no before your uncle's land come to me to know how to direct a letter to you and that is concerning Cousin Jane Bray's business. I shall be like a fool to double my request to you that I might hear from you, and that I might know how to direct my letters to you, for I do fear that they do not come to your hand. Your brother Hooper and his wife, and your sister Marcy, desired to be remembered to you and yours. Your uncles and aunt doth the same; my kind respects to Cousin Jane Bray and her family; not else at present but my prayers constantly to the Lord for you, & remain your loving mother, JANE GAYER.

From Plymouth, this 11 June, 1694.
These for Mr. William Gayer.
Living on the Island of Nantucket, New England.

NOTE —I heard during the present month, February, 1877, from a lady, a descendant of William Gayer, Esq, that when her mother was very young, some seventy years ago probably, news came to Nantucket that a very large property in England had been left for descendants of the Gayer family. Thomas Starbuck of Nantucket was desirous his son Joseph, a very smart business man, should go to England to investigate the matter; but he felt he could not spare the time it would require, so he, with his older brothers, Simeon and Levi, sent over an agent to Great Britain, who returned and reported he had not carried out sufficient documents and there the case ended, as far as Nantucket interest was concerned.

WILLIAM C. FOLGER.

(*William Gayer, Sen., to his daughter Damaris Coffin, wife of Capt. Nathaniel Coffin.*)

DAUGHTER DAMARIS,

These may serve to inform you we are all well. When I wrote you your mother Coffin was designed to Boston by Land I find I was mistaken. She tells me since her intent was only to the main. Christian is now at her grand ffather Coffins. Mr. Folger came home from Boston yesterday and informs me that John Sowters brother came from England lately, and says he spoke with your brother William G. in the East Indies Eighteen months since. If you have a convenient opportunity I wish you would speak with him and inquire what you can about William. I hope you will let me hear from you as often as you have opportunity for I take great Delight to hear of your welfare so with my love to yourself and Children with all other friends I remain your father

WILLIAM GAYER NANTUCKET Septr· 9 · 1709.

Mr Nathaniel Coffin | in | Charls Towne.

In a letter from Thomas and James Hooper to William Gayer, Nantucket, dated "Stone house, near Plymouth, the 15th of February, 1699–70," they say, "Mother desires to be remembered unto all." His wife had been sick about six months. They had heard by his son William from their brother William, of Nantucket, nothing else important.

(*Mrs. Damaris Coffin, wife of Captain Nathaniel Coffin and daughter of William Gayer, Esq., of Nantucket, to her uncle, Sir John Gayer, then in the East Indies.*)

BOSTON, N. E. 10th Jan ye 1711–12.

MOST HON^D UNCLE

Inclosed is a copy of what my husband wrote you in his last, advising you of the death of my hon^d father y^{or} brother William Gayer & of the Disposition we had made of our son William &c to which refer you.

I have now before me the hon^r of your kind letter of the 5th Jan'ry 1709–10. Directed to my deceased father.

The Good Character and Hopeful State of my brother with you is very reviving and the more Comfortable seeing you Express an Inclination to send him for Brittain, and in hopes you will soon follow him yourself. For which Blessing I daily Elevate my Prayers to my God, That he would Bless prosper and protect you both and send you to the height of your desires therein in health and safety.

My son goes on hopefully with his book I am in hopes that God will bless you and send you Safe to yo' native Country, and will prepare my boy to wait on you to your content and Satisfaction, whenever you please to put your Commands on him So to do. My Good Husband hath met with hard Fortune in his last voyage from Lisboa being taken and Carried into France, where he hath been a Prisoner a long time and was not released in   last but was in hopes to procure his Liberty in a short time and go for London from whence probably you may hear from him. He has been from home now for months and when he will be set free which is uncertain. God direct him and us for the best. I must conclude with my Duty to you & my true respects to my brother if with you & am most sincerely   Hon^d Uncle

   Your most affec"

   NIECE.

(Sir Isaac Coffin to Jona Amory of Boston)

CHARLESTON, 12th May, 1817.

MY DEAR COUSIN:

Letters from England, received yesterday, oblige me to leave this country much sooner than was expected, for I fully intended at least to pass a week with you, prior to my departure. Inclose to you the Secret of the accumulation in the American Funds and beg your kind attention as far as is convenient to my Magdalen Island concerns.

The inclosed for Messrs T. Belcher and Wright will explain to you what my intentions are, and the remittances you may expect from that Quarter.

It will be necessary you should by some careful person remit the certificates of the stocks to me under cover to Messrs. Thos. Wm. Earles Co., Liverpool, taking the proper precaution by notarial copies or otherwise as you may judge best, and you may continue to draw on Messr. Thos. Coutts & Co., Strand, London, until the interest in the 7 and 6 yrs Cents, amounts to three hundred sterling, *adding* to it any remittance you may receive from Messrs. Belcher and Wright, and the interests of the Stock already invested as it becomes payable, until further order.

The 10th of January and 10th of July, one hundred and twenty-five pounds, are at each period, paid into my bankers' hands. The 10th of

April and 10th of October, two hundred and fourteen pounds are received by them. Manage the time of drawing for these sums periodically, and that the bills may be presented with regularity. The half pay in advance quarterly, may be drawn by you, as it becomes due.

Bill the 1st of July, £167; October 1st, £167; 1st January, £167; 1st April, £167. I will on my arrival in England, immediately prepare my banker for this arrangement; and now for the Secret, it is for a Charitable Institution, so as you are known to be one of the best of men, help me as well as you can. Thanks for your offer of credit, I shall have no occasion at present for it.

Most truly do I lament this unforseen event has deprived me of the pleasure of seeing you, your family, and my friends.

Remember me kindly to them all, my aunt and Dr. Dexter.

By some kind master forward my baggage to Liverpool, that is in your custody and believe me

Ever Affectionately yours,   ISAAC COFFIN.

(*To Commodore Hull*).

LONDON, 5 May, 1819.

MY DEAR SIR:

Long, very long, have I been expecting the huge Lobster you were so kind as to promise me. "Better late than never." I send you a simple contrivance for   to examine the   when you have as many line of Battle Ships as we have its application may be useful.

A Petition against my return to Parliament was presented to the House, and, in the event of my being thrown out, it was my intention to take a trip again across the Ocean and visit my friends at Boston; but, by a Resolution of the Committee, I am reseated, my Opponent having

I must, therefore, now defer my voyage to some more favorable opportunity In any way that I can be useful to you here, I pray command me. Offer my best wishes to your spouse and all friends.

Believing me very truly yours,

ISAAC COFFIN.

P. S. When you have the goodness to write me, send the letter via Liverpool, the lobster to the care of Col. Aspinwall. Address to the care of Messrs. Tho. and Wm. Early & Co, Liverpool

ADMIRAL COFFIN.

LONDON, 3rd June, 1818.

MY DEAR SIR:

In looking over some old charts, I found one of Boston Harbour which, though of an ancient date, may still be correct. It shows the state of the Town, when the troops of Great Britain were shut up in it, and most of the surrounding Forts, Dorchester excepted.

I beg your acceptance of it, and when placed in your office it will serve to remind you of one who holds you in high estimation.

Offer to your spouse and her lovely sister my best wishes, and believe me always, yours very truly,

ISAAC COFFIN.

CAPT. HULL

LONDON, 16th April, 1819.

MY DEAR SIR:

My reputation will sink to the lowest ebb, unless your efforts are crowned with success relating to the Lobster. Should you fail to cross the Ocean again, I long to try my luck by travelling in the Bay between Cape Cod and Cape Ann. I lament the situation I hold prevents me paying you a visit this Spring, as my Spirits were never better, and the *Gout not within hail*

Remember me kindly to your spouse and all my relations.

Truly yours,

ISAAC COFFIN.

CAPTAIN HULL, Boston.

LONDON, May 20th, 1819.

MY DEAR SIR:

Allow me to offer for your acceptance the Telegraph.

With my new occupation little time is left me to look into a Signal Book. Besides, there is little chance of ever being employed again, and certainly none in fighting against that country that gave me birth. If at your leisure moments you can pick out anything that may be useful or ornamental, I shall be gratified.

Should one of those huge lobsters be forthcoming, remember that you do not forget me. In looking over some papers the other day, I found some charts of old Massachusetts, which may one of these days find their way to you.

Kind remembrances to all friends.

Always Yours Truly,

ISAAC COFFIN.

CAPTAIN I. HULL.

LONDON, 13th July, 1819.

MY DEAR SIR:

The lobster you committed to the care of Captain Tracy arrived in good condition. It is considered a marvellous one here. Still, my friend, Sir Joseph Banks, longs for one of ninety pounds, which your letter speaks of, so that you must be on the lookout still for me; and should you be successful in procuring another of uncommon size, you must have the goodness to forward it, taking care first to boil it in strong pickle or brine; then it will become dry in the interior very soon, and bear being moved about with greater facility. I have been offered by some showmen a large sum, but I decline parting with him, intending it for a Lady's Museum. A Hodge-Podge, as you will perceive in the Signal line, was months since deposited with Col. Aspinwall; but no opportunity has offered of sending it before Captain Tracy's arrival. I am too old to pry into modern curiosities, never meaning to serve again against friend or foe, but do as much good as I can for the rising generation, who may, when I am under ground, fight it out in any way most convenient to the parties.

I have this winter fired a shot now and then, avoiding close action, as I soon observed, like our Dr. Sewell's Meeting-House in Summer, many members fast asleep during long and tedious harangues, in the House of Commons. I thought at first the sound of my own voice would have alarmed me before such an audience. Having had occasion often to address my ship's company gave a facility at first setting off, so that when blowing hard I did not broach to or get becalmed while delivering my sentiments to the House. Nothing will give me more pleasure than once more meeting my old friends at Boston, a town I shall ever regard as long as my heart is left to beat.

Kind remembrances to your spouse, Nat Amory, and all the other worthies. Believe me always

Very Faithfully Yours,

ISAAC COFFIN.

CAPT. I. HULL.

LONDON, 26 Jan., 1819.

MY DEAR SIR:

There is an old sea song I used to sing when creeping in Boston Bay during the Revolutionary War, in the months of January and February, "What cannot be cured must be endured."

Many thanks for kind exertions. Send the Lobster when you can. My reputation will be saved, though my money is gone; consign it to the care of your Consul to whom I have written on the subject, and remember in return if you do not command my services in a way that I can be useful to you it will be your own fault. Any intelligence you can afford me will be most interesting, especially on nautical or agricultural subjects. I have taken my seat in the House of Commons, and may one of these days be instigated to speak, but at present play the part of "Orator Mum." Remember me kindly to your spouse, Nat Amory, and all friends in Boston, believing me always, my dear Captain,

Very truly yours,

ISAAC COFFIN.

CAPTAIN ISAAC HULL, Naval Commissioner, Boston.

(To General Dearborn.)

LEININGTON SPA, 23d July, 1827.

MY DEAR SIR:

Please to accept my thanks for your kind recollection of my wishes. The Terrapin you had the goodness to send me is in the safe custody of my friend William Earle at Liverpool. As many more as you can pick up in your garden, except the small speckled ones and snappers, will be acceptable. The latter are such determined deserters that no bounty or kind treatment will keep them loyal. In early life I have seen a large sort with a rough bark resembling those brought by your whalers from the Gallipagos Islands. I beg you to present my kind regards to all my Boston friends. Sink or swim I never can forget the place of my nativity or cease to wish prosperity to it.

Ever my dear Sir truly yours,

ISAAC COFFIN.

GENERAL DEARBORN.

(*General John Coffin, to Stephen De Blois, of Boston.*)

ST. JOHN'S, N. B., Feb. 10, 1830.

MY DEAR STEPHEN.

You are now from various unforeseen and melancholy changes that have taken place in your circle of very dear friends, left as almost the sole survivor. Time and chance sets all adrift. I truly condole with you and them in the loss of so many excellent and worthy characters. Boston will never be to me what it has been—not that my affections has in any degree abated for those remaining. Such however being the will of Providence, we must submit with becoming patience and fortitude, looking forward to the time when it will be our turn to follow I am passing the winter in this frozen region, and what with good friends and good cheer, I am, thank Providence, enabled to carry a weather helm, and maintain a tolerable share of health I hope this may find you and Mrs. Deblois and family enjoying health and comfort, and that all my friends and relations are doing the same. I hardly dare ask for our old and respectable friends, Dr. and Mrs Dexter; to them and my friend Tom and wife with their branches, remember me in the kindest terms; also to Mr. and Mrs. Davis, Mrs Smith, and good little Maynard

Does Mrs. T C. Amory continue to be your neighbor? To her and charming family, with Mrs. Jona and their family, my kind love and affections.

There is also Mr John Amory, the worthy Doctors of Old Trinity, Gardiner Greene, with many others that I love in my heart, and it gives me pleasure to name them, and let them know that I do not forget them, and the comfort and gratification I have enjoyed in a long and early acquaintance and friendship I am fond of this plain old fashioned way of keeping alive those cheering recollections of the past happy days, and the absent. I am with them as far as the most kindly feelings towards them can be allowed to exist. Have you any late accounts from our worthy cousin Nat and wife, Capt. and Mrs Derby, friends and associates rare to be met with in this or any other hemisphere. Are they allowed to hold their appointments under your new President, whose vacillating conduct has, I understand, changed the position of many in politics. I never meddle with but I must say this much, I do not envy your constitution and government

Aside and between ourselves, what has induced Sir Isaac to desert the country that has conferred on him the rank and consequence he now enjoys? Were the American people any way behind those of Great Britain in nautical tactics, he might gain some applause But I am sure every well thinking man with you must condemn him for deserting the country that has conferred on him even more than he had any right to expect or look for. I am afraid his fair fame and character will be much clouded on the other side of the water from which he will never recover. I should not be surprised to hear his Majesty had struck his name out of the list of Admirals. The injury will unfortunately extend to every branch of his family connected with the service in which we are all engaged. I cannot but say I am deeply wounded at this not to say more inconsiderate conduct He must have taken leave of his senses It is, however, too painful a subject to dwell on, and I shall conclude my dear cousin, with the kindest regards to all the De Blois, and remain your very attached,

JOHN COFFIN.

JUNE, 1719.

DEAR COZ:

Yours I received, with the half crown and am sorry you should have troubled yourself about so small a matter; that or any command should have been observed without such punctualities. I ask a thousand pardons for my long silence; my lady Duchess having been for some time indisposed that I could not gain this opportunity sooner. I have taken the following accompts, from the worthies of Devonshire, out of our office; and, for those of Hants, they shew the exact arms of the seal of my formers, which was my father's, given by him to one Mr. James Coffin, of Christ Church, Hants, in whose possession it is. I observe those of Hants spell with the letter (y), those of Devonshire, as you see My shortness of time will not allow of any regard to stops, and scarcely orthography, so beg your excuse for all faults, as well as a line just to satisfy me of your receipt of this This day, se'nnight, or to-morrow, his Grace intends for Nottingham, Lancashire, and York; so that if you have any commands to communicate, I shall be proud to bear them; and am with all respect (my mother and sister's services attending you),

Madam, Your most humble servant,

RICHARD COFFYN.

For MRS MARY COFFIN, at Ramsdon Heath, in Essex.

[ARMS.]   FLOR., A.D. 1533
                                R. R. HEN. 8.

These letters afford some partial glimpse of the writers, and the times in which they lived. They are presented in connection with the memoirs of Sir Isaac, that his kinsfolk or collectors of autographs who possess any letters of his own, or which may shed light on his career, may be disposed to send the originals or copies to some central and accessible repository, where they can be kept together for the benefit of other generations. The fireproof vaults of the New England Genealogical and Historical Society, 18 Somerset Street, in Boston, where he was born, are suggested as a fitting Place.

XX.

THE COFFIN SCHOOLS.

The letter to his cousin, p. 88, shows that Sir Isaac had determined to establish in Massachusetts a system of nautical schools—one for Boston, one for Newburyport, and another later at Nantucket. Having had occasion to learn, when in our city council and on our school board, how very general an impression then existed of the importance of thus building up our commercial marine, it seemed due to the memory of Sir Isaac to comprise in this memoir the sketch of what he intended his schools should be. Mr. Folger, who possesses what seems a copy of the original draught of a will of his, in which he had himself set forth his plan, permits me to use it. The admiral, from his own experience as a midshipman and forty years in service, more or less active in the navy, had an experience which gives value to his ideas of nautical education.

The Clio was bought, equipped, and used some years, and no doubt educated many excellent seamen. His kinsman, Hector, of the Newburyport branch of the Coffins, was in many ways well fitted to take charge. It will be seen that ten years after the inception of the plan, the Clio was still employed in the task. It involved more cost than was contemplated, and was given up about the time Sir Isaac founded the Coffin school at Nantucket, which, with means largely accumulated, is in a full career of usefulness, though somewhat modified in its methods and scope from what the founder contemplated

The plan for the nautical schools is thus set forth in the will, revoked, if it still existed, when he made his last will the year that he died.

THIS IS THE LAST WILL AND TESTAMENT OF ME, SIR ISAAC COFFIN, BARONET, an Admiral in the service of his Majesty George the Fourth, King of the United Kingdom of Great Britian and Ireland.

I direct all my just debts and funeral expenses, and the costs and charges of proving this my will, to be paid And holding in grateful remembrance the manifold blessings I have derived from the principles instilled into me while at Boston, in the State of Massachusetts, the place of my nativity, and feeling that the success I have experienced in this life is mainly to be attributed to the excellent education I received at that place, and wishing that none of my relations, being lineal descendants of Tristram Coffin, who settled in the township of Salsbury, near Newbury Port, in the said State of Massachusetts, in or about the year one thousand six hundred and forty-two, and of Peter Coffin, his brother,* and bearing or taking the name of Coffin, may ever want the means of obtaining those advantages so bountifully bestowed on me, I give and bequeath all the personal property of which I may be possessed, or to which I may be entitled at my death, in possession, revision, or expectantly, to my executors hereinafter named, in trust, to transfer the same to seven trustees, to be appointed as hereinafter provided, for the establishment of three schools for naval education, one at said Boston, one at Nantucket, in the State of Massachusetts, and one at said Newbury Port. And for the purpose of maintaining and perpetuating such establishments according to this, my last will, I do appoint five visitors or overseers of the said trust ; that is to say · whoever shall be, for the time being, successively the governor of the said State of Massachusetts, the president of Harvard University at Cambridge in the said State, and the Mayor of the said city of Boston, with two others to be chosen by the said three ; and the said visitors shall have the power to fill all vacancies that shall occur in their own body, whether by death or resignation of any visitor that may be chosen as aforesaid, or from the discontinuance or other change of either of the said three officers.

Item : I do authorise and request the said visitors, as soon as may be after my decease, to nominate and appoint seven discreet and faithful persons to be Trustees for the establishment of the said three schools , and if they shall not make such appointment within one year after this my will shall have been duely proved and allowed, then I authorise and request my Executors to appoint the said seven Trustees, and the said Trustees, when appointed in either of the modes above mentioned, shall forever thereafter fill all vacancies in their own body, their election in each case to be submitted without delay to the said visitors for their approbation, and to be void if disaproved by the visitors , and if the Trustees shall refuse or neglect to fill any such vacancy for the space of three months after the same shall occur, and for the same length of time after being notified of the vacancy by the visitors and being requested by them to proceed to a choice, then the said visitors are authorised and requested forthwith to fill such vacancy by the appointment of a Trustee. And I do further authorise the said visitors, from time to time, to remove any of the said Trustees

---

* His son

who shall in the opinion of the visitors become incapable or unfit by reason of age, infirmity, or any other cause to discharge the duties of his office.

Item · I do order and request my Executors hereinafter named, as soon as may be after my decease, to pay over, deliver, assign, and transfer to the said Trustees all my said personal estate herein above bequeathed to the said Trustees, to be held by them upon the trusts and for the purposes following; that is to say: all that part of my said estate which may at the time of my decease be invested in the British funds to be kept to accumulate by investing the interest from the time in the like stock, and adding it to the principal, for sixty years after my decease, if the rules of law or equity will allow it, otherwise, for any less time than sixty years that shall be allowable; and if from any cause it should become impracticable or greatly disadvantageous to the said establishment to keep the last-mentioned part of my estate invested as aforesaid in the British funds, then I authorise the said Trustees, with the consent and approbation of the said visitors, to withdraw the whole of said monies from the British funds, and invest the same in other stocks or funds, or in real estate, or put the same out at interest to be accumulated as aforesaid, as they shall think best for the establishment, and in either case, when the said fund shall cease to be accumulated as aforesaid, whether by force of the above-written limitation or of the rules of law, it shall be appropriated, together with the other property herein bequeathed to the said Trustees, to the maintenance of the said schools, as hereinafter provided, and as to the residue of my said estate, bequeathed as aforesaid (as also the part thereof last above mentioned, when the said trust for accumulation shall cease), the said Trustees shall from time to time invest the same in any stocks or funds, or in real estate, or put the same out at interest, as shall be warranted and allowed by law, and shall appear to be secure and most for the advantage of the said establishment, and if it shall hereafter appear to the said Visitors and Trustees that the property herein given to the said Trustees can be better managed and secured. and the purposes of this my will be better attained, by an incorporation of the said Trustees and Visitors, or either of them, I do hereby, so far as in me lies, assent to such incorporation, and do request that the same may be granted accordingly by the competent authority of the said State of Massachusetts on the application of the said Visitors and Trustees. And the said Trustees shall have the care and immediate oversight of the said schools, and may make all necessary and proper rules and regulations for the discipline and instruction and the general government thereof, provided they be not inconsistent with the regulations in that behalf contained in this my will, and all such rules and regulations shall be in full force and operation until repealed by the said Visitors

Item: I will and direct that each of such schools shall be on the following plan and Foundation, viz.: Each to be called "Sir Isaac Coffin's School." One of such schools, being the school to be first established, to be at Boston, in such a situation that the scholars may be near the water-side and have ready access to the Harbour. The school to consist of twenty-four scholars; twelve of them, if so many may be found, are to be the male descendants, deriving their descent through males of the said Tristram Coffin, and of said Peter Coffin, respectively, or one of them, and to bear, or before entrance into the school, to take and assume the name of Coffin. If male relations, deriving their pedigree through males, should not be found, then descendants by the female line may be chosen, and they to assume and bear and write the name of Coffin before they enter into the school. And I direct that such twelve scholars of each school shall be fed, clothed, and lodged out of the income of the funds of the establishment And I direct that three masters be appointed for each school, viz.: a Master of a Ship, a Mathematical Master, and a Drawing Master, each to be of good Morals and reputation and well qualified for his department. Such three persons will, in my humble judgment, be sufficient to prepare the boys for the profession they are designed to follow. And I direct that the remaining twelve boys of the school at Boston shall be selected from the sons of honest and industrious inhabitants of Boston who may be desirous of breeding up their sons for a nautical life. And it is further my will that the sons of the poorest citizens shall be preferred, and that no boy shall be eligible who shall have any bodily deformity, or who shall not be of a sound constitution, or who shall not have had the small-pox, or have been vaccinated. It is further my will that no boy shall be admitted until he shall have attained the age of fourteen years, and that each boy should be able to read, and also to write a legible hand, and have a competant knowledge of Arithmetic, and be of Christian persuasion, and if a classical scholar, he is on that account to be entitled *caeteris paribus* to preference. Each boy shall leave the school at the age of eighteen. And I direct that the Ship Master, Mathematical Master, and Drawing Master should respectively be native citizens of Massachusetts.

Item: As my said property may not be sufficient to found the three schools to commence at the same time, I direct the school at Boston to be first established, and as the funds accumulate, to form the second of such establishments at Newbury Port. And, as future funds accumulate, to form the third and last of such establishments at Nantucket. And I direct that each of such schools shall be conducted on similar plans, and each school to be limited to the number of twenty-four boys, and all the boys beyond the twelve of the Coffin family to be chosen by the Trustees out of the respective Towns in which such schools are to be established; and on failure of that number, then to be selected from any other part of the State of Massachusetts. But this shall not prevent the Trustees from admitting additional scholars on payment of such sums for their tuition as the Trustees shall prescribe, when it can be done without injury to the establishment. And, whereas the branches of the family of the said Tristram Coffin and Peter Coffin are spread over the Continent of North America and Europe, and are my relations, I direct that any of them, and of whatever country they may be natives, shall forever be eligible to be placed in each of the said schools, the number of twelve such relations being always entitled to the preference to be scholars on each of such foundations when of a proper age, and if such relations can be traced; and the said Trustees shall have the exclusive right and power of certifying the fact of descent and right of eligibility And I direct that for the admission of each boy, an application shall be made to the said Trustees three calendar months before he can be admitted upon any vacancy, and that the day of admission shall be the sixteenth of May in every year (being the anniversary of my birthday) And I direct that no candidate shall be admitted unless a physician and surgeon, to be appointed by the said Trustees, shall certify to them, after due examination, that such candidate is, as to bodily health, fit for the life of a Sailor. And I direct that, as between different applicants for admission, the said Trustees, or the major part of them, shall have the selection and choice, and that proximity of blood among persons of the sirname, or being descendants from the said Tristram Coffin and Peter Coffin, respectively, shall not confer any right of preference. And I direct that, adjacent to each school, a house should, if it be deemed expedient, be obtained by purchase or hiring on lease, and furnished for the residence of the Ship-Master of each school. And I direct that the Ship-Master for each School shall have the direction, care, and superintendence of the said boys on that foundation to which he shall be attached, and of their board and lodging, and his board and lodging gratis in the same house. And I direct that his accounts of expenditure for board and lodging shall be submitted to the annual inspection of the Trustees, and that the Trustees (should there be occasion) may, with the assent of the Visitors, remove any of the said Masters for misconduct or want of qualification.

Item: For promoting the welfare of the said establishment, I direct that for each of the said schools a sloop of fifty tons, coppered and copper fastened, shall be built or provided at the expense of the establishment, combining strength, convenience, fast sailing, and durability, and furnished with bed-places and all requisite conveniences for the scholars; and that the scholars of the Boston foundation shall be exercised in cruising in Massachusetts Bay and the neighboring coast, from the tenth day of May to the tenth day of September in each year, by which means they will become excellent pilots, and they are to be put into and survey all the harbors from Passamaquoddy to Nantucket, and to trawl and drudge on every part of the coast, and on all occasions, to try to discover the treasures of the deep; and to keep an accurate journal of their proceedings, and use their fishing-lines, of every kind, when opportunity may offer, and, by keeping the body and mind in constant activity, they will prepare themselves for the arduous career incident to the life of a seaman, and they are not to lose any opportunity of making astronomical and nautical observations. The sloop to be caulked and kept in repair and sails, rigging, and hull, by the personal labor of the masters and scholars, and to be called "The Seaman's Hope," carrying a white flag with a pine-tree in the centre. And I direct that the boys, in the two first classes of each establishment, shall be exercised two years in the sloop of such establishment prior to leaving school. And I direct that the sloop belonging to the Newbury Port School shall cruise from Cape Cod, round Boston Bay to Passamaquoddy, and that the sloop belonging to the Nantucket School shall cruise from Cape Cod one way, to New York the other way, trawling and drudging assiduously as the ground will admit, since I conceive many oyster-beds may be discovered in Long Island Sound, and between Montauck Point and Sandy Hook. And it is my further direction that the boys of each school shall, from their entry to their departure, wear a blue jacket and trousers of good cloth of the second or third quality, with blue knit stockings of worsted in winter, and cotton in summer, and shall have an anchor on the right arm, of red cloth, by which they may always be known and distinguished. And as the vessel may go into the Bay in severe weather, I direct that a competent number of greatcoats be provided, lined with baize made up of No. 4 canvas and painted, and also foraging leather caps to cover their heads, and with a small anchor in front of each cap. Also, that the boat be provided and hoisted up at any wharf in the vicinity of each school at which permission may be obtained, and rowing twelve oars double-banked, and having cork apparatus sufficient to float her when overset, and in that boat the two junior classes of each school shall be exercised from the tenth day of May to the tenth day of September in each year, thus combining exertion with pleasure. And I direct that each of the scholars shall learn to swim, and each acquire a knowledge of the following trades or callings— that is to say Ship-building, caulking, rope-making, block-making, mast-making, boat-building, coopering, house-carpenter's and joiner's work, baking, blacksmith's work, cutting and making clothes, knitting, making nets of all kinds, mixing paints and painting, the art of cooking in all its branches, the art of slaughtering animals with due economy, also of preserving meat by pickling, salting, or smoking. I also direct that muskets be provided and kept up, to belong to each school, that the boys of the first class may be exercised by the Ship-Master, at such time as he may think most convenient, in firing at a mark, and such guns always to be cleaned and put by by the scholars of the said class And I direct that the scholars be taught the use of the backsword, the art of gunnery, and firelock exercise, and be at liberty to amuse themselves at proper times with athletic games, such as cricket, foot-ball, wrestling, at the discretion of the Ship-Master and Mathematical Master, one of whom is always to be in attendance on the scholars as their charge And I will and direct that each boy shall be at his studies at five o'clock in the morning in the summer, and at six o'clock in the morning in the winter. The scholars to be at breakfast at seven o'clock in the summer, and at eight o'clock in the winter, and winter is to be reckoned to commence from the first day of November and to end on the thirtieth day of April. The boys to dine at one o'clock in the summer, and to be allowed one hour and a half for the interval between school, to dine in winter at one o'clock, and to be allowed one hour between school, and to have two half-holidays in each week, commencing from one o'clock; the boys on the foundation who shall not have any relations in town, to be regulated as to their absence by the Ship-Master; and all the boys to sup in winter and summer at eight o'clock and be in bed by nine. Their food to consist of rice, Indian meal, and bread, with milk and molasses or sugar, for breakfast, mutton, beef, pork, and fish, with potatoes and other vegetables and soups, according to the judgment of the Ship-Master, for dinner, and in such proportions as may be equal to the several wants of the boys, avoiding waste and profusion. The boys to have for supper the same kind of food as for breakfast.

Item · I will and direct that the said Trustees shall visit and examine the said school in Boston at least four times a year, and oftener if they think proper, and I do request that the said Visitors join in such examination at least once a year; and I further authorize and request the said Visitors to depute and appoint the respective School Committees, or Selectmen, for the time being, of the said towns of Nantucket and Newbury

Port, or such other persons as the Visitors shall nominate, to make a like visitation and examination of the schools in those towns respectively, and to report their observations to the said Visitors, in order that all defects in the course of discipline and instruction in the said three schools may be discovered and corrected, and that such improvements may be made therein, by the said Trustees and Visitors, as they shall judge proper, and not inconsistent with the general object and plan of the schools as expressed in this my Will. And in case of the misconduct of any scholar which cannot be sufficiently punished or repressed by the ordinary discipline of the school, the Trustees may, on complaint by the Mathematical Master or Ship-Master, inquire into the same, and, if they think proper, admonish the scholar; and on a second complaint, they may sentence him to a short solitary confinement; and if this should prove inefficient, such boy may be expelled; or any boy may be expelled in the first instance for any aggravated offence that shows him to be wholly unworthy of enjoying the benefits of the school, and no boy once expelled shall ever be reinstated.

Item. As the Lancasterian or Bell system of education has, in most countries, been found very beneficial, I should wish the schools to be regulated as nearly as possible on that plan, or any improvement thereon. And I direct that in each school there may be four classes, and the boy most conspicuous for talents and proficiency in each class to be placed at the head of that class as a monitor. Each boy of the senior to have a boy of the second class to instruct, and each boy of the second class to have one of the boys of the third class to instruct, and each boy of the third class to have a boy of the fourth class to instruct By these regulations knowledge will be rapidly diffused, and the education of the young men sooner completed. I wish the boys to be in every respect as well qualified in mathematical and astronomical knowledge as the scholars at the Naval College at Portsmouth, in England, are qualified, and to complete the like plan as is observed in that academy. And I will and direct that each Mathematical Master, in addition to his other qualifications, should be competent to give lectures on the several heads of natural philosophy, namely, pneumatics, hydraulics, optics, mechanics, electricity, astronomy, geology, geography with the use of the globes; and that a philosophical apparatus should be provided at the expense of each establishment And I direct that each school should be provided with Ree's Encyclopædia, printed and published in America, and a competent number of books which treat or may treat on professional matters I direct also that models of a ship, brig, snow-schooner, and sloop be provided in each school, and that the boys may be practised in rigging and unrigging the same during the winter. And I recommend that shops be built near the school wherein the different trades enumerated for the boys to learn may be taught. I also direct that Arrowsmith's Mercator's chart of the world, and spherical chart, together with maps of the four quarters of the globe, should be hung up on springs in each school, so that ready access can be had to the maps, and that a pair of globes should be provided for each school. And I direct that, when either of the said schools should be complete, and the boys of the senior class be about to leave it, an examination should take place touching their abilities, when all the Selectmen and Magistrates, Captains and Officers of the United States Navy residing at Boston, Newbury Port, or Nantucket, and respectable Masters of ships should, by public advertisement, be invited to attend. And after such examination I direct that each boy, on leaving the school, should, if merited, have a mark of approbation, *i.e.*, the first boy a silver medal, and I direct that the silver medal shall have engraved on one side a ship completely rigged with a motto, "I aspire to command," and on the other side "God is my Guide," with a wreath of laurel and a sextant; the second boy a sextant; the third boy a quadrant, the fourth boy a case of mathematical instruments, the fifth boy a treatise on Navigation, the sixth boy the book called "A Coasting Pilot," or the best substitute for it; and if there be any more, the seventh boy a fishing-line of sixty fathoms with lead and six cod-hooks; the eighth boy a chest for his clothes; the ninth boy a Gunter's scale and a pair of compasses, and each of the others a jack knife; each boy also to have a Bible, and a certificate, signed by the Ship-Master and the Mathematical Master, that he was educated at Sir Isaac Coffin's School. And I direct that a proper book be kept by each Ship-Master by way of registry of the names of all the scholars, stating their ages and their respective proficiency in the sciences taught at each school, such book, together with the plans and drawings of the boys who may excel, to be preserved in the library of the school. And it is my direction that the Ship-Master of each school shall be thirty years of age before he shall be qualified to conduct the affairs of the establishment, and shall not be eligible after the age of forty-five years, and that he may, if he think fit, or be required by the Trustees to, retire at any time after the age of sixty, with an annuity for his life of fifty pounds sterling per annum. And that the Mathematical Master shall not be admitted after the age of thirty years, and may retire at any time after sixty years, if he should so desire, or be required as aforesaid, with an annuity of fifty pounds for his life. The Drawing-Master to be admitted at any age between twenty-one and forty-five years, and may retire at any time after sixty, if he should so desire or be so required, with an annuity for his life of forty pounds per annum

Item : Having suggested, so far as my experience enables me, the requisites for forming a set of men who may be useful to my native country, my consideration has been to provide the funds for establishing the said Foundation. I have at present, standing in the names of the Trustees of my marriage settlement, which, after the death of my wife, will be part of my property, about seven hundred pounds a year in the English Funds, and in my own name six hundred pounds a year in the Funds of the United States, and money and stock in the French Funds, which sums may be more or less, and I may considerably increase them in my lifetime. Should the income of the funds be adequate after what is above disposed of, I direct that sums not exceeding fifty pounds per annum should be given to each of twelve aged and infirm Masters of Merchant Ships, who may be worn out and unable to support themselves, at Boston, Nantucket, or Newbury Port, giving the preference to the descendants of Tristram Coffin and Peter Coffin in the male or female lines. And should there be any surplus fund after supporting and maintaining the aforesaid three establishments, and after paying the said annuities to the said twelve aged and infirm Masters of ships, I direct that such surplus be given, by way of annual income, for the maintenance of the aged and infirm branches, members for the time being of the Coffin family from the said two stocks, in such a way and proportion as the said Trustees may adjudge.

Item . I revoke all other wills made by me at any time heretofore. And I nominate, constitute, and appoint Jonathan Amory and Henry Codman, both of said Boston, Esquires, William Appleton, Jonathan Amory, Jun., Thomas Coffin Amory, Edward Gardiner Davis, M.D., George Minot Dexter, William Davis Sohier, Edward William Payne, and Thomas Amory Deblois, all of said Boston, Esquires, to be Executors of this my Will and Testament, and desire that all their expenses may be borne and paid out of my estate.

In Witness Whereof I have, to this my last Will and Testament, contained in eight sheets of paper, set my hand and seal (that is to say), my hand only to the first seven sheets, and my hand and seal to this the eighth and last sheet, this fourth day of September, in the year   of the reign of George the fourth, and in the year of our Lord one thousand.

Signed, sealed, published, and declared by the said Testator as and for his last Will and Testament, in the presence of us, who at his request and in his presence, and also in the presence of each other, have hereunto subscribed our names as witnesses.

BOSTON, 16th Sept., 1829.

MY DEAR SIR:

No event of my life has ever afforded me more pleasure than my late visit to Nantucket—and as you have, from the commencement of my efforts to form the establishment for our young relations, mainly contributed thereto, I beg once more to offer you my best thanks.

But for *you*, probably, we should *never* have witnessed the affecting and gratifying exhibition of the children at the seminary

You will hear I have taken much interest in the equipment of the Brig, giving the boys plenty of pumpkins, squashes, apples, and good advice. They go to their work with a *hearty* good *will*. I pray God they may make good men They clear out this day, and sail to-morrow. Little or no gout since we parted. I start for New York to-morrow. Early in November go to Norfolk, thence to South Carolina Kind regards to your family, the Trustees, your son, and the children, and *all* relations

Ever sincerely yours,

WM. COFFIN, ESQ. (Signed)   ISAAC COFFIN.

The nautical schools involving too large an expenditure, and having, as his brother John writes his cousin Stephen Deblois, provoked criticism at home, Sir Isaac directed his attention to establishing a school at Nantucket. This still exists, well endowed. Its pupils, once two or three hundred, are not now confined to the descendants of Tristram. It is said of this school that it cost Sir Isaac an earldom, but the remark applies with more likelihood to the nautical schools for the education of seamen. The following letter to the trustees of the Nantucket school from Mr. Folger, who sends me the above intended will, is appended, with his consent.

CAMBRIDGEPORT, June 30, 1881.

CHARLES G. COFFIN, ESQ., *President Board of Trustees,*
   Admiral Sir Isaac Coffin's School, Nantucket:

MY DEAR AND HONORED FRIEND—Some few years ago, in looking over old records in the " Town's Building," so called, at Nantucket, I came across a candle-box about half filled with loose papers. On examination I found among them several original letters and memorandum-books connected with the establishment of the Coffin School. By permission I took them for the purpose of making copies tending to their preservation. I infer that they were saved when all the other records of the School were destroyed by the fire of 1846, conveyed from the counting-room of the Secretary, Gorham Coffin, Esq, to his residence, and at his death carried over to the Town's Building. But this, being my own explanation, may not be the correct one. The papers consist of two books of accounts, showing the purchase and fitting the School House on Fair-Street, and the general expenditures from September, 1826, to May, 1835 ; four memorandum books containing the names of scholars, male and female, commencing with the first quarter of the second year, June, 1828, and continuing to March, 1834, and sundry documents numbered by the Secretary, Gorham Coffin, Esq., 1 to 81—of which 22 were missing—and there are 9 not numbered. They consist of original letters from Admiral Coffin and his relative, Hector Coffin, to William Coffin, President of the Board of Trustees , copies of letters to the Admiral, and copies of papers connected with the gift by Union Lodge of F. & A. Masons, under certain conditions, of their Lodge Building standing on Main street. These documents I have carefully copied into a record book, and, in connection therewith, other information connected with the establishment of the school, showing some of the influences leading thereto, together with such biographical notices of Admiral Coffin as have come under my observation. It appears that on the 10th of September, 1826, Admiral Coffin visited Nantucket a second time, after an interval of about twenty years. He found the inhabitants very much exercised in relation to the establishment of public schools. The only schools of this nature then existing were charity schools, supported by the Town from an appropriation of $1,500 per year, with an expenditure of about $800 in a population of some 8,000 persons. The School Committee of 1825 had reported " that they had not recommended a large sum of money, because it is presumed that no individual who is competent to support the education of his children, will at this period of embarrassment be induced to place them under the direction and control of the School Committee "

The names of those participating in the appropriation were required to be published by the Committee. At the March Town Meeting, 1826, the School Committee reported, "that immediately after their appointment they gave public notice that they would be in session to receive applications for admission into the public schools. They sat several evenings for the purpose, and until applications had ceased. Having ascertained by this course the number of children for which they had to provide schools, they proceeded to institute schools, and locate them in different parts of the town for the accommodation of the inhabitants ; one under the direction of a master, and four under the direction of mistresses. These schools have embraced, on an average, about 180 scholars Besides these five schools, provision has been made for a few scholars in four private schools, in such a manner that it has been advantageous to the scholars themselves, and economical to the town. The Committee have frequently visited the schools in order to take cognizance of any existing difficulty, as well as to ascertain the advancement of the schools in their several studies, and to this end have examined every individual scholar. The condition of very many of the scholars," say the committee, " was indeed deplorable at the time they were received, and although their advancement has generally equalled the most sanguine expectations of your committee, yet very much remains for the town to do, that the education, which, in many instances, received its beginning the present year, may be continued, till an object fraught with the most beneficial effects shall be fully accomplished. One of the above female schools is composed of colored children, whose advancement in education has afforded satisfaction to the Committee, when they have visited the schools. They have expended $845 94, and have drawn $650, and there is due to the treasurer $194 94 They recommend the like appropriation of last year, $1,000, with liberty to hire $500 more if necessary. And in conclusion, recommend the t)wn so far to reconsider a vote of last year as to dispense with publishing the names of each individual who has participated the last year in the appropriation." In the meantime the columns of the Nantucket *Inquirer* were teeming with powerfully-written articles, showing the necessity and express duty of the town to adopt a public school system The able and talented editor, the lamented Samuel Haynes Jenks, in sharp and incontrovertible statements showed that the schools supported by the town were strictly and only "charity" schools for the destitute, and not in any sense public schools ; that although the Commonwealth had passed laws more than thirty-five years previous for tne general education of youth, yet no provision in accordance had ever been made by the town of Nantucket, and that no legal public school then existed in the place.

At the session of the General Court held in 1826 additional laws were passed in relation to public education and the establishment of schools for this purpose by the several towns. At the same session an act was passed, approved March 2, 1826, establishing sessions of the Supreme Judicial Court in the county of Nantucket, and at its first session the inhabitants of the town were indicted for neglect of schools, whereupon notice was issued to the said inhabitants and the case continued to the next term of the Court, on the first Tuesday of July following, 1827.

At the height of this excitement Admiral Coffin visited Nantucket, and undoubtedly his attention was drawn to the "deplorable condition" of some of his young kinsmen, as described by the school committee of the town, and he was induced to carry into execution a plan he had long had in contemplation—the establishment of a school upon the Lancasterian system, designed for the youthful descendants of whatever name, of Tristram Coffin, his ancestor, who first emigrated from England and settled in Saulsbury near Newburyport, and in 1661 removed to Nantucket and there spent the remainder of his days The Coffin school was opened on the 29th day of May, 1827, and on the same day two public schools by the town of Nantucket, which, at the previous March meeting, had appropriated for the purpose $2,500. The Nantucket *Inquirer* of June 4th records that "on Monday last, two of the large public schools recently established by a vote of this town were opened for the admission of scholars These seminaries, which will contain an aggregate of nearly 350 scholars, were immediately filled with children above the age of nine years. It is ascertained that about 300 younger candidates for public instruction now remain to be provided for. The schools now established are to be conducted on the improved monitorial plan. The Principal Schools in this town are as follows: South public school, under the direction of Mr. William Mitchell, containing 202 scholars. North Public School, under the joint care of Messrs. Nathaniel and Obed Barney, 143 scholars at present. Admiral Sir Isaac Coffin's Lancasterian school, conducted by William Coffin, Jr., and Miss A. Meach, comprising 230 scholars." This noble institution, founded in 1827, has extended its benefits not only to the descendants of Tristram Coffin, but to the children of Nantucket generally for a period of more than fifty years, increasing in usefulness with its years, and bidding fair to continue to an indefinite period of time. While disasters and misfortunes without number have fallen thick and heavy upon the old town, while her children have been driven to the ends of the earth to earn a livelihood, while her wharves have fallen in decay, the grass grown in her streets, and the sound of labor become low or ceased altogether, yet this grand old institution, founded in love and good will, standing almost alone, has flourished and grown strong amid a general wreck.

The prophetic words of the Boston *Evening Bulletin* on the foundation of the Coffin School seem to be fulfilled, and the lesson therein inculcated is worthy our serious consideration at the present time: "When it is recollected that in the compact town of Nantucket, comprising a population of nearly eight thousand, there were, two years since, no seminaries for the public instruction of youth ; and that upon the establishment of the institution in question, designed for the benefit of a numerous class of the community, the town itself, provoked and ashamed, as it were, by this magnanimous example, was incited to the erection of three similar schools, what thanks will not be awarded by the future inhabitants of that island; what magnificent results to coming generations may not be justly anticipated. This is the way to insure immortal fame ! This is the judicious and generous mode which Admiral Coffin has adopted for the transmission to after ages of the remembrance and the benefits of his bounty, instead of vainly providing for the erection of marble monuments or bestowing his wealth for the propagation of sectarian doctrines."

My connection with the school was as a pupil at the second quarter in the second year, and I had the honor of receiving a first medal in the boys' school at the end of the fourth quarter. I was a pupil when the school was visited by Admiral Coffin in 1829, and recollect being playfully taken upon his knee at visits he made at my grandfather's at that time. I was also a member of the Board of Trustees several years, where we had always the pleasure of your company and the benefit of your advice and co-operation, which you have so freely and generously given through the entire existence of the school, having been one of the original Board of Trustees appointed by the Admiral, and for many years the only surviving member thus appointed, and distant is the day, all must join in wishing, when your connection therewith shall cease. The great obligation I feel to the school of my early days, through which I stumbled with weak and faltering steps, but to which distance lends a sweet enchantment, has led me to ask the acceptance by the Trustees of this book of records which I take the liberty to forward to you with the original papers before mentioned I also ask their acceptance of one of the original medals, struck off by direction of Admiral Coffin in memory of Tristram Coffin, the first of his race that settled in America, and copies of which he sent to the members of the first Board of Trustees. This medal was given to me by the late Paul Mitchell, Esq., an acquaintance and near relative to the great Admiral.

With my best wishes for the continued prosperity of the school, and assurance of my high regard and esteem to yourself and the other Trustees I am, very respectfully,

Your friend and ob't servant,

GEORGE H. FOLGER.

GLEANINGS.

CONTENTS OF GLEANINGS.

	PAGE
John	115
Turbot	117
Haverhill	118
Nantucket Deeds	119
Papers connected with Government of Nantucket	124
Tristram's Deeds to his Children	129
Number of Tristram's Descendants	135
Obituary of Admiral Sir Isaac Coffin	136
List of Vessels to which Admiral Coffin was attached	139
Conclusion	140

"JOHN."

P. 57.

As our memoir was on its way to the corner bookstore, in search of a reader, a friend, whose boyhood had been spent in Brighton, recalled to remembrance a character too intimately associated with the admiral to pass unnoticed. His Yes, Sir Isaac, No, Sir Isaac, recurring at every sentence, as he received his master's orders, still reëchoes on the ear. Thoroughly English in appearance, speech, and dress, his spatterdashes, corduroys, jockey coat, and cap with a gold band somewhat tarnished, worn as a badge of his master's rank in the British navy, attracted attention the more that our people then scrupulously refrained from any such pretensions. His manners, warm and magnetic with his equals, deferential to those he regarded as his superiors, were rather domineering over the stable-boys who served under him. If, like a true Saxon, he used or dropped his aspirates somewhat erroneously, he was, when at ease, loquacious and sensible, and left the impression that he was thoroughbred for his peculiar walk.

Exuberant in health, his well-knit frame solid and muscular, half-sailor, half-groom, he had the credit of being besides an accomplished personal attendant, either as valet, nurse, or butler, as the occasion served. In earlier days, in his capacity as master's man, then deemed indispensable to all personages of means, military rank, or social position, he had attended Sir Isaac about the world, afloat or ashore. On an occasion like that of the Nore, when the admiral one stormy night plunged into the wintry billows to save a drowning sailor, John, at the imminent risk of his own life, had rescued his master from the sharks. Such a service the admiral was not likely to forget.

However extended his social circle, numerous his acquaintances and friends, and frequent a guest under many hospitable roofs, ever ready to receive him with cordial welcome, Sir Isaac, without domestic ties or other home than his cabin, had often to lead a lonely life. He had few dependants in whom to take an interest, for whose welfare and happiness he felt under obligation to care. One in whom he placed implicit trust, who in so many ways contributed to his own comfort, intelligent and respectful, yet companionable, and who had rendered him such excellent service on the occasion to which we have alluded, occupied a high place in his regard to their mutual advantage.

His special charge, when, at this suggestion of my friend, the substantial presence of John stalked sturdily back into my own consciousness, was the stable at Brighton, near the hall on the hill-top, then standing in lonely dignity against the sky but long since removed, of the Massachusetts Agricultural Society. In its spacious stables, befitting their antecedents, the victors of Epsom and Ascot and of other well-known courses, imported by Sir Isaac to improve our breeds, reposed upon their laurels, or transmitted them to other generations. In buildings round about frolicked their progeny of frisky and comely foals. John, well-versed in horse-flesh, an admirable veterinary surgeon, watched with parental solicitude over these precious animals committed to his care, ambitious to bring them up in the way they should go.

The Society in whose keeping the horses had been placed, and under whose sanction and auspices the benevolent purposes of the admiral were carried out, then reigned in solitary supremacy. The numerous county organizations were not in existence. Its annual fairs attracted crowds from all over New England. Its members were from among the most eminent of the State. Still remembered well the day when Sir Isaac, who was then residing not far away, at Belmont, then my uncle's, where we also had our dwelling, attended as their guest. His presence there, and that of these fine steeds confided by him to their care, was an event, and John, as master-of-horse, in his glory.

Naturally generous, and ever thoughtful of the wants of whoever had any claim upon him, the admiral purchased a farm of many acres near the stables at Brighton, and gave it to John. There, with his buxom wife and healthy children, still clinging to the ways and customs of England, he lived on long past maturity, if not to a great old age. His chief pride as long as they remained here, for they eventually went back to England, were the horses, and with them he shared the regard of his neighbors, many of whom had profited by the opportunity and possessed themselves of scions of such illustrious sires. Two splendid colts of Barefoot's were killed by lightning when pastured on an island in the harbor. Morgan and other breeds, better adapted to hard work and the intensities of heat and cold, superseded Barefoot's; but doubtless still may be traced on the famous Brighton road near by, his fleetness and elegance of form grafted on more sturdy stock.

Our climate, with such extremes of temperature often abrupt, is better suited for wheel or runners than for the saddle. Population crowding along shore has well-nigh exterminated the fox and deer, and the chase without useful purpose lost much of its fascination. Even racing is becoming confined to trotting in harness. But when Sir Isaac sent over Barefoot and Serab to improve our stock, New England, like the Old, had not lost its taste for running. There were other champions of the turf to be remembered besides Winslow Blue Foxes, too, abounded up to the suburbs of our larger municipalities. Well-mounted clubs of the best and wealthiest, for their extermination, in traditional splendor of apparel, leaped the stiff stone walls that bounded the fields, as much for their own enjoyment as for the benefit of the farmers. Even at this day, at Newport and Beverly, men and women gather in large numbers to the meet, with well-trained hunters and dogs of high degree, though Reynard rarely puts in an appearance, and a bag of aniseseed in a cart proves a sorry substitute.

Our late civil war quickened the taste for equitation. Spacious parks gird round our cities or compose large portions of their extended areas. Attractive drives, well-shaded, by the sea or through the forest about our summer resorts, tend to promote a taste once more common abroad than here. What we still need are better horses for the saddle, from stocks with hereditary aptitudes, well-trained till training becomes second nature. The best will then become more abundant, and be less costly. Other public benefactors will introduce from abroad, or other parts of our own land, choice breeds for the purpose, acclimatize them here, teach them their paces, and to apprehend instinctively the intent of the rider Then the Boston boy, who did so much half a century ago in this same direction, will be appreciated and held in grateful remembrance by all, who estimate aright the healthy exhilaration of speeding through the air on a perfect mount.

TURBOT.

P 57.

It is a curious fact that deep-water fish, soles and turbot, change gradually through their generations, — change not only their accustomed habits and habitats, but their form and color, to accommodate themselves to their new conditions and perils. On the different sides of a broad channel, of the broad ocean between Europe and America, the mouth opens sometimes on one side and sometimes on the other, according to the slope of the shore. Our American turbot, if not equal in flavor or delicacy to its English congener, is very similar in general appearance, but with sufficient modifications of form not to be mistaken for it. Sir Isaac had been so constantly from early childhood in constant proximity to the sea in climates so various, that he was conversant with all the innumerable tribes of the ocean, and, realizing how much better the English turbot was than ours, he brought over, on one of his voyages, in crails both turbot and sole, in the hope they might in time become acclimatized and multiply in our waters. Our own fishermen say that the English turbot has occasionally, though rarely, been caught here retaining in large measure the delicacy and other characteristics of the race. Possibly with time they will gradually, by selection of breed, and for self-preservation, conform more to our type, yet be a better fish. Our chicken halibut, and the larger variety, good and abundant, leave, however, little more to be wished.

HAVERHILL.

"It appears that Tristram did not affect a permanent settlement at Salisbury, but removed the same year to the new settlement of Pentucket, soon afterward called Haverhill. This settlement was commenced in 1640, Christopher Hussey being among the first settlers, but no deed from the Indians was obtained until 1642, when the name of Tristram Coffyn appears as one of the witnesses thereto. It was first recorded in the county records of Norfolk (lib. 2, p. 209); and, in 1832, the original deed was said to be in the possession of Charles White, Esq. As it is the first appearance of the name of Tristram Coffyn upon any document in America, I make a copy of it from the 'History of Haverhill,' by B. L. Mirick. The marks made by the Indian sachems were representations of the bow and arrow: —

'Know all men by these presents that we, Passaquo and Saggahew, with the consent of Passaconaway, have sold unto the inhabitants of Pentucket all the lands we have in Pentucket, that is, eight miles in length from the little river in Pentucket westward; six miles in length from the aforesaid river northward, and six miles in length from the aforesaid river eastward, with the island and the river; that the island stand in as far in length as the land lies by as formerly expressed, that is, fourteen miles in length. And we, the said Passaquo and Saggahew, with the consent of Passaconnaway, have sold unto the said inhabitants all the right that we or any of us have in the said ground and island and river, and we warrant it against all or any other Indians whatsoever unto the said inhabitants of Pentucket, and to their heirs and assigns forever. Dated the fifteenth day of November, A. D. 1642

Witness our hands and seals to this bargain of sale the day and year above written We, the said Passaquo & Saggahew, have received in hand, for and in consideration of the same, three pounds and ten shillings.

In the presence of us

  John Ward.
  Robert Clements,
  Tristram Coffyn,
  Hugh Sherratt,
  William White,
   The sign of (1)
  Thomas Davis.

The mark of
Pasaquos X [Seal].

The mark of
Saggahew, X [Seal].'

Tristram Coffyn settled in Haverhill near Robert Clement, and tradition says he was the first person who ploughed land in that town, constructing his own plough. The following year he settled at the Rocks, so called. He resided in Haverhill several years, when he removed to Newbury (1648-9), and thence to Salisbury (1654-5), where he organized the company for the purchase and settlement of Nantucket"

NANTUCKET.

Ch. iv, p 21.

"These documents, printed thirty years ago from the records of New York at Albany, are not accessible to many who may read this volume. Some of them are of value as showing by what conveyances Nantucket and Martha's-Vineyard vested in the colonists. Others have peculiar interest at this time that systems of government for dependencies, or for associated nationalities, are under discussion. The plan evidently originated on the islands. What part of it was the work of Mayhew, Coffin, or Macy, does not appear. They probably all participated, and were alike competent to adapt sound political methods and principles to the circumstances and exigencies with which they had to deal.

Deeds from James Fforrett to Thomas Mayhew and Son
[Deeds, i, 71; iii, 64, and iii, 76, Secretary's Office, Albany.]

These presents do witness, That I, James Fforrett, gentleman, who was sent over into these parts of America, by the Honorable Lord Sterling, with a commission for the ordering and disposing of all the islands that lie between Cape Cod and Hudson river, and have hitherto continued his agent without any contradiction, do hereby grant unto Thomas Mayhew at Watertown, merchant, and to Thomas Mayhew his son, free liberty and full power to them, their heirs and assigns, to plant and inhabit upon Nantucket, and two small islands adjacent, and to enjoy the said islands to them, their heirs and assigns forever. Provided, that Thomas Mayhew, and Thomas Mayhew his son, or either of them or their assigns, do render and pay yearly unto the Honorable the Lord Sterling, his heirs and assigns, such an acknowledgment as shall be thought fit by John Winthrop, Esq., the elder, or any two magistrates in the Massachusetts Bay, being chosen for that end and purpose by the Hon. the Lord Sterling, or his deputy, and by the said Thomas Mayhew and Thomas Mayhew his son, or their assigns

It is agreed, that the government that the said Thomas Mayhew, and Thomas Mayhew his son and their assigns shall set up, shall be such as is now established in the Massachusetts aforesaid, and that the said Thomas Mayhew, and Thomas Mayhew his son, and their assigns shall have as much privilege touching their planting, inhabiting, and enjoying of all and every part of the premises, as by the patent to the patentees of the Massachusetts aforesaid, and their associates In witness hereof, I, the said James Fforrett, have hereunto set my hand and seal this 13th day of October, 1641.

            JAMES FFORRETT. (Seal)
Witnesses: PHILIP WATSON, *Clerk*
 ROBERT CORANE,
 NICHOLAS DAVISON,
 RICHARD STILLMAN.

A Deed made to Mr. Mayhew by Richard Vines.
[Deeds, iii, 66, Secretary's Office.]

I, Richard Vines, of Saco, gentleman, steward-general for Sir Ferdinand Georges, Knight, Lord Proprietor of the province of main land and the islands of Capairock and Nantican, do, by these presents, give full power and authority unto Thomas Mayhew, gentleman, his heirs and associates, to plant and inhabit upon the islands of Caparrock, alias Martha's Vineyard, with all rights and privileges thereunto belonging, to enjoy the premises unto himself, his heirs, and associates forever, yielding and paying unto the said Sir Ferdinand Gorges, his heirs and assigns, forever annually, as two gentlemen, indifferently by each of them chosen, shall judge to be meet by way of acknowledgment.

Given under my hand this 25th day of October, 1641.

RICHARD VINES.

Witness:
THOMAS PAGE,
ROBERT LONG.

Deed of Nantucket to ten Purchasers.

[Deeds, III, 56, Secretary's Office.]

Recorded for Mr Coffin and Mr. Macy aforesaid the day and year aforesaid.

Be it known unto all men by these presents, that I, Thomas Mayhew, of Martha's Vineyard merchant, do hereby acknowledge that I have sold unto Tristram Coffin, Thomas Macy, Christopher Hussey, Richard Swayne, Thomas Bernard, Peter Coffin, Stephen Greenleafe, John Swayne, and William Pike, that right and interest I have in the land of Nantucket, by patent; the which right I bought of James Fforrett, gentleman, and steward to the Lord Sterling, and of Richard Vines, sometimes of Saco, gentleman, steward-general unto Sir Gorges, knight, as by conveyances, under their hands and seals, do appear, for them the aforesaid to enjoy, and their heirs and assigns forever, with all the privileges thereunto belonging, for and in consideration of the sum of thirty pounds of current pay, unto whomsoever I, the said Thomas Mayhew, my heirs or assigns, shall appoint. And also two beaver hats, one for myself and one for my wife. And further, this is to declare that I, the said Thomas Mayhew, have reserved to myself that neck upon Nantucket called Masquetuck, or that neck of land called Nashayte, the neck (but one) northerly of Masquetuck, the aforesaid sale in anywise notwithstanding. And further, I, the said Thomas Mayhew, am to bear my part of the charge of the said purchase abovenamed, and to hold one-twentieth part of all lands purchased already, or shall be hereafter purchased, upon the said island by the aforesaid purchasers or heirs and assigns forever. Briefly, it is thus: That I really sold all my patent to the aforesaid nine men, and they are to pay me, or whomsoever I shall appoint them, the sum of thirty pounds in good merchantable pay in the Massachusetts, under which government they now inhabit, and two beaver hats, and I am to bear a twentieth part of the charge of the purchase, and to have a twentieth part of all lands and privileges, and to have which of the necks aforesaid that I will myself, paying for it; only the purchasers are to pay what the sachem is to have for Masquetuck, although I have the other neck.

And in witness hereof, I have hereunto set my hand and seal this second day of July, sixteen hundred and fifty-nine (1659).

Per me, THOMAS MAYHEW.

Witness:
    JOHN SMYTH,
    EDWARD SCALE.

Deed of Tuckanucket Island.

[Deeds, iii, 57, Secretary's Office.]

Recorded for Mr. Coffin and Mr. Macy aforesaid, the day and year afore written.

The tenth day of October, one thousand six hundred fifty-nine. These presents witness, that I, Thomas Mayhew, of Martin's Vineyard, merchant, do give, grant, bargain, and sell all my right and interest in Tuckanuck Island, alias Tuckanucket, which I have had or ought to have, by virtue of patent right purchased of the Lord Sterling's agent, and of Mr. Richard Vines, agent unto Sir Ferdinand Gorges, Knight, unto Tristram Coffin, Sr., Peter Coffin, Tristram Coffin, Jr., and James Coffin, to them and their heirs forever, for and in consideration of the just sum of six pounds in hand paid, and by me, Thomas Mayhew, received in full satisfaction of the aforesaid patent right of the aforesaid island.

And in witness hereof I have set my hand and seal

Per me, THOMAS MAYHEW.

Witness hereunto:
    ROGER WHEELER,
    GEORGE WHEELER.

Deed of Wanockmamack.

This witnesseth that I, Wanochmamack, chief sachem of Nantucket, hath sold unto Mr Tristram Coffin and Thomas Macy, their heirs and assigns, that whole neck of land called by the Indians, Pacummohquah, being at the east end of Nantucket, for and in consideration of five pounds, to be paid to me in English goods or otherwise to my content by the said Tristram Coffin aforesaid, at convenient time as shall be demanded Witness my hand or mark this 22d of June, 1662.

WANOCKMAMAK.

Witness hereto.

PETER FOLGER & WAWINNESIT whose English name is Amos

Indian Deed of Nantucket.

[Deeds, iii, 54, Secretary's Office.]

Recorded for Mr. Tristram Coffin and Mr. Thomas Macy, the 29th of June, 1671, aforesaid.

These presents witness, that I, Wanackmamack, head sachem of the island of Nantucket, have bargained and sold, and do by these presents bargain and sell, unto Tristram Coffin, Thomas Macy, Richard Swayne, Thomas Bernard, John Swayne, Mr. Thomas Mayhew, Edward Starbuck, Peter Coffin, James Coffin, Stephen Greenleafe, Tristram Coffin, Jr, Thomas Coleman, Robert Bernard, Christopher Hussey, Robert Pike, John Smythe, and John Bishop, these islands of Nantucket, namely, all the west end of the aforesaid island, unto the pond commonly called Waquittaquay, and from the head of that pond to the north side of the island Manamoy, bounded by a path from the head of the pond aforesaid to Manamoy; as also a neck at the east end of the island called Poquomock, with the property thereof, and all the royalties, privileges, and immunities thereto belonging, or whatsoever right I, the aforesaid Wanackmamack have, or have had in the same; That is, all the lands aforementioned, and likewise the winter feed of the whole island from the end of an Indian harvest until planting time, or the first of May, from year to year forever; as likewise liberty to make use of wood and timber on all parts of the island; and likewise half of the meadows and marshes on all parts of the island, without or beside the aforesaid tracts of land purchased; and likewise the use of the other half of the meadows and marshes on all parts of the island, without or beside the aforesaid tracts of land purchased; and likewise the use of the other half of the meadows and marshes, as long as the aforesaid English, their heirs and assigns, live on the island; and likewise I, the aforesaid Wanackmamack, do sell unto the English aforementioned, the propriety of the rest of the island belonging unto me, for, and in consideration of forty pounds already received by me, or other by my consent or order. To have and to hold, the aforesaid tracts of land, with the propriety, royalties, immunities, privileges and all appurtenances thereunto belonging to them, the aforesaid purchasers, their heirs and assigns forever.

In witness whereof, I, the aforesaid Wanackmamack, have hereunto set my hand and seal, the day and year above written.

The sign of WANACKMAMACK.

Signed, sealed, and delivered in the presence of
    PETER FOULGER,
    ELEAZER FOULGER,
    DORCAS STARBUCK.

Indian Receipt for Land — Receipt of Wanackmamack.
[Nantucket Records, Old Book, page 27.]

Received of Tristram Coffin, of Nantucket, the just sum of five pounds which is part of the seven pounds that was unpaid of the twenty pound purchase of land that was purchased of Wanackmamack and Neckanoose, that is to say, from Monomoy to Waquettaquage pond, Nanahumack neck, and all from Wesco westward to the west end of Nantucket, I say, received by me, Wanackmamak, of Tristram Coffin, five pounds sterling, the 18th of the eleventh month, 1671.

The X mark of
WANACKMAMACK.

Witness hereunto:
    RICHARD GARDNER,
    ELEZER FOLGER.

Two Letters or Certificates from the Inhabitants of Nantucket.
[Deeds, iii, 58, Secretary's Office, Albany.]

Recorded for the aforesaid Mr Coffin and Mr. Macy, two lives on certificates, from the inhabitants of Nantucket, as follows, viz.: —

Whereas, the Honorable Colonel Lovelace, Governor of New York, gave forth his summons for the inhabitants of the isle of Nantucket to make their appearance before His Honor at New York, either in their own person or by their agent, to show their claims in respect to their standing or claim of interest on the aforesaid island. Now we, whose names are underwritten, having intrusted our father, Tristram Coffin, to make answer for us, we do empower our father, Tristram Coffin, to act and do for us with the honored Governor Lovelace, so far as is just and reasonable, with regard to our interest on the isle of Nantucket and Tuckanuckett.

Witness our hands the second day of the fourth month, sixteen hundred and seventy-one (1671).

JAMES COFFIN,
NATHANIEL STARBUCK,
JOHN COFFIN,
STEPHEN COFFIN.

This is to signify that the inhabitants of Nantucket have chosen Mr. Thomas Macy their agent to treat with the Honorable Colonel Lovelace concerning the affairs of the island, to act for them in their behalf and stead, and in all considerations to do what is necessary to be done in reference to the premises, as if they themselves were personally present.

Witness their hands, dated June 5, 1671.

EDWARD STARBUCK,
PETER FOLGER,
JOHN ROLFE.

The inhabitants aforesaid do also, in the name of the rest, desire Mr. Tristram Coffin to assist their aforesaid agent what he can in the matter or business concerning the Island Nantucket.

Proposals to the Governor from the Inhabitants of Nantucket about Settling that Government.

[Deeds, III, 59, Secretary's Office.]

Imprimis. We humbly propose liberty for the inhabitants to choose annually a man or men to be chief in the government, and chosen or appointed by His Honor to stand in place, constantly invested with power of confirmation, by oath or engagement, or otherwise as His Honor shall appoint, one to be chief in the court and to have magistratial power at all times with regard to the peace, and other necessary considerations.

Second. We take for granted that the laws of England are standard of government, so far as we know them, and are suitable to our condition, yet we humbly propose that the inhabitants may have power to constitute such law or orders as are necessary and suitable to our condition not repugnant to the laws of England

Third. In point of carrying on the government from time to time, we are willing to join with our neighbor island, the Vineyard, to keep together one court every year, one year at our island, the next with them, and power at home to end all cases not exceeding twenty pounds; and in all cases liberty of appeal to the general court in all actions above forty pounds. And in all actions amounting to the value of one hundred pounds, liberty of appeal to His Highness, his court at the city of New York, and in capital cases, or such matters as concern life, limb, or banishment. All such cases to be tried at New York.

Fourth. And feeling the Indians are numerous among us, we propose that our government may extend to them, and power to summon them to our courts with respect to trespass, debt, and other miscarriages, and to try and judge them according to laws, when published amongst them.

And, lastly, some military power committed to us respecting our defence, either in respect of Indians or strangers invading, etc.

The Answer to the Nantucket Proposals.

[Deeds, III, 60, Secretary's Office.]

At a council held at Fort James, in New York, the 28th day of June, in the twenty-third year of His Majesty's reign, Anno Domini 1671.

In answer to the proposals delivered in by Mr. Coffin and Mr. Macy on the behalf of themselves and the rest of the inhabitants upon the Island Nantucket, the governor and council do give their resolutions as follows, viz. —

Imprimis. As to the first branch in their proposals it is thought fit that the inhabitants do annually recommend two persons to the governor, out of which he will nominate one to be the chief magistrate upon that island, and the island of Tuckanuckett, near adjacent, for the year ensuing, who shall, by commission, be invested with power accordingly.

That the time when such a magistrate shall enter into his employment after the expiration of this first year shall commence upon the 13th day of October, being His Royal Highness's birthday, to continue for the space of one whole year, and that they return the names of the two persons they shall recommend three months before that time to the governor.

That the inhabitants have power by a major vote annually to elect and choose their inferior officers, both civil and military, that is to say, the assistants, constables, and other inferior officers, for the civil government, and such inferior officers for the military as shall be thought needful.

Second. The second proposal is allowed of: That they shall have liberty to make peculiar laws and orders at their General Court for the well government of the inhabitants, the which shall be in force amongst them for one whole year, during which time, if no inconvenience do appear therein, they are to transmit the said laws or orders to the governor for his confirmation. However, they are (as near as may be) to conform themselves to the laws of England, and to be very cautious they do not act in any way repugnant to them.

Third. To the third it is granted that they join with their neighbors of Martha's Vineyard in keeping a General Court between them once a year, the said court to be held one year in one island, and the next year in the other, where the chief magistrate in each island where the court shall be held is to preside, and to sit in their respective courts as president, but, withal, that upon all occasions he counsel and advise with the chief magistrate of the other island.

That the said General Court shall consist of the two chief magistrates of both islands, and the four assistants, where the president shall have a casting voice; for the time of their meeting, that it be left to themselves to agree upon the most convenient season of the year

That in their private courts at home, which are to be held by the chief magistrate and two assistants, where the chief magistrate shall have but a single voice, they shall have power finally to determine and decide all cases not exceeding the value of five pounds without appeal; but in any sum above that value they have liberty of appeal to their General Court, who may determine absolutely any case under fifty pounds without appeal; but if it shall exceed that sum the party aggrieved may have recourse, by way of appeal, to the General Court of Assizes, held in New York.

And as to criminal cases, that they have power both at their private courts at home, as well as at the General Court, to inflict punishment on offenders so far as whipping, stocks, and pilloring, or other public shame. But if the crime happen to be of a higher nature, where life, limb, or banishment are concerned, that such matters be transmitted to the General Court of Assizes likewise.

Fourth. In answer to the fourth, it is left to themselves to order those affairs about the Indians, and to act therein, according to their best discretions, so far as life is not concerned, wherein they are also to have recourse to New York, but that they be careful to use such moderation amongst them that they be not exasperated, but by degrees may be brought to be conformable to the laws; to which end they are to nominate and appoint constables amongst them who may have staves with the King's arms upon them, the better to keep their people in awe and good order, as is practised with good success amongst the Indians at the east end of Long Island.

To the last, that they return a list of the inhabitants, as also the names of two persons amongst them; out of whom the governor will appoint one to be their chief military officer, that they may be in the better capacity to defend themselves against their enemies, whether Indians or others.

Nantucket Affairs.
[Deeds, iii, 85, Secretary's Office.]

Additional instructions and directions for the government of the Island Nantucket, sent by Mr. Richard and Captain Jno. Gardner, April the 18th, 1673.

Imprimis, that in regard that the town upon the island of Nantucket is not known by any peculiar or particular name, it shall from henceforth be called and distinguished in all deeds, records, and writings by the name of the town of Sherborne, upon the Island Nantucket.

That all ancient and obsolete deeds, grants, writings, or conveyances of lands upon the said island, shall be esteemed of no force or validity, but the records of every one's claim or interest shall bear date from the first divulging of the patent granted to the inhabitants by authority of His Royal Highness, and so forward, but not before the date thereof.

That the time of election of the chief magistrate, and other civil officers, be and continue according to the directions and instructions already given; but in regard of the distance of the place and the uncertainty of the conveyance betwixt that and this place, the chief magistrate and all the civil officers shall continue in their employments until the return of the governor's choice and approbation of a new magistrate be sent unto them, which is to be with the first convenient opportunity.

That in case of mortality, if it shall please God the chief magistrate shall die before the expiration of his employment, the assistants for the time being shall manage and carry on the affairs of the public until the time of the new election, and the governor's return and approbation of a new magistrate in his stead.

That the chief military officer shall continue in his employment during the governor's pleasure, and that he have power to appoint such persons for inferior officers as he shall judge most fit and capable.

That in case of the death of the chief military officer during the time of his employment, that then the inhabitants do forthwith make choice of two persons, and return their names unto the governor, who will appoint one of them to be the officer in his stead.

That in regard to the General Court to be held in the Island Nantucket or Martha's Vineyard is but once in the year, where all causes or actions are triable without appeal to the sum of fifty pounds, liberty be granted to try all actions of debt or trespass at their ordinary courts to the value of ten pounds without appeal, unless upon occasion of error in the proceedings there, because of complaint from the ordinary court unto the General Court, or from the General Court to the Court of Assizes.

That what is granted in the general patent to the inhabitants, freeholders of the Island Nantucket, is to be understood, unto them alone who live upon the place and make improvement thereof, or such others who having pretences of interest shall come to inhabit there.

Given under my hand at Fort James, in New York, the day and year afore written, and in the twenty-fifth year of His Majesty's reign.

Soon after the marriage of Mary Coffin, the youngest daughter of Tristram, with Nathaniel Starbuck, the old gentleman concluded to make his son-in-law a landed proprietor, and, with as much care for the contingencies of the future as kind parents exercise in the present age, and with equal nicety in the choice of language as may be found in modern conveyances, executed the following deed to his daughter and her husband. It will be seen that it was made some years before it was acknowledged, and acknowledged some years before it was recorded: —

Tristram conveys to daughter, Mary Starbuck, and her husband, Nathaniel, one-half of all estates.

[Nantucket Records, 1st Book, Page 97.]

Know all men by these presents, that I, Tristram Coffin, of Nantucket, do for divers good considerations, as also in regard of my fatherly affections, do give unto my daughter, Mary Starbuck, the one-half of my accommodation of my purchase, on Nantucket Island, namely, the half of my tenth part which I bought with the other nine first purchasers of Mr Thomas Mayhew, in patent right, and of the Sachems Indians right, as by their grant in the deed will at large appear. I do as aforesaid give and grant unto my daughter, Mary Starbuck, all the one-half of my accommodation of patent right, and all my right of the half of all lands, meadows, marshes, commons, timber, wood, and all appurtenances thereunto belonging, as fully as myself or any of the other twenty part shares have or ought to have, in manner and form following: the one-half to her own and her husband's disposal, namely, her husband, Nathaniel Starbuck, to them and their heirs and assigns, forever, the other half to my aforesaid daughter, Mary Starbuck, and Nathaniel Starbuck, her husband, during their lives, and when they die, then it shall be for the use of my daughter, Mary Starbuck's child, or children, to him, her, or them, and their heirs, forever, but if my daughter, Mary Starbuck, have no child or children living when she dieth, then it shall be in the power of her husband, Nathaniel Starbuck, to dispose of all the aforesaid lands and accommodations, with all appurtenances, as he shall judge most meet. In witness whereof, I, the said Tristram Coffin, have hereunto set my hand and seal, this 14th fourth month, 1664.

Tristram Coffyn.

[Signed, sealed, and delivered in the presence of —
Thomas Macy,
Mary Swain,
Sarah Macy.

This deed was acknowledged before me, Thomas Mayhew, upon the island of Nantucket, this 15th day of January, 1677; I say before me,

Thomas Mayhew, Mag

July 26, 1736. — Then received the original of this above written deed, and by the desire of same concerned, perfected the record above by making the sign of the seal. Attest:

Elezer Folger, Regr.

While Tristram was generally reputed to be quite wealthy in goods and lands, owning, together with his sons, at one time about one-fourth part of the island of Nantucket and the whole of Tuckernuck, he did not die rich. He fully realized that he could not take his riches with him to another world, and that the amount of land he would require at his death would be very small. He made no will, but disposed of much of his land while he lived, by deeds, the consideration always being his ' regard and natural affection.' Most of the remainder of his estate he deeded to his two youngest sons, John and Stephen, and they were to take after the decease of both himself and his wife. To each of his grandchildren he gave ten acres of land upon the island of Tuckernuck, or to such of them as would plant it.

Tristram to Stephen, his youngest son, conveying half his accommodations, excepting his new house on the hill.

[Nantucket Records, Old Book, Page 63.]

Know all men by these presents that I, Tristram Coffin, of Nantucket, Senior, do give, grant, bargain, and sell unto my son, Stephen Coffin, the one-half of my land at Cappam, alias Northam, within the township of Sherborn, situated upon Nantucket island, that is to say, the one-half of my house lot, with half my accommodations and privileges and appurtenances whatsoever thereunto belonging, all buildings, except that is to say, my new dwelling-house upon the hill, and my old dwelling-house under the hill, by the herb-garden; now, for and in consideration of the aforesaid premises, my son, Stephen Coffin, shall always from time to time do the best he can in managing of my other half of my lands and accommodation during mine and my wife's life, and that he be helpful to me and his mother in our old age and sickness, what he can: now I, Tristram Coffin, abovesaid, do for this and for divers other considerations me moving thereunto, do, as abovesaid, give, grant, bargain, and sell unto my son, Stephen Coffin, his heirs and assigns, all my one-half of my house lot, with all appurtenances thereunto belonging: To have and to hold forever, to him, the said Stephen Coffin, his heirs and assigns, executors and administrators, upon the conditions aforesaid: and my son, Stephen Coffin, shall always, from time to time, have free liberty to go to and fro to the new barn that he hath lately built with horse, foot, and cart, as he hath occasion, and to have the free use of half an acre of land adjoining the said barn on the east side, and south and north side. In witness whereof I have set my hand and seal, the fifteenth of the eleventh month, one thousand six hundred and seventy-six. TRISTRAM COFFYN.

Acknowledged before me the deed within written this 15th day of June, 1677. THOMAS MAYHEW,
Magistrate.

Agreement between Stephen Coffin and his father, as to rights in barn to Tristram and his wife Dionis.

[Nantucket Records, 2d Book, Page 12.]

Articles of agreement between Tristram Coffin, Senior, and Stephen Coffin, son of the aforesaid Tristram Coffin, both of the town of Sherborn, on the island of Nantucket, as follows: imprimis, we do jointly and severally agree that whereas there is a barn built at Coppamet by us, this present year, one thousand six hundred seventy-seven, that the aforesaid Stephen Coffin had been at the most part of the charge, therefore I, Tristram Coffin, do covenant and agree with my son, Stephen Coffin, that he shall have the aforesaid barn and lean-tos for himself, and his heirs and assigns, forever, to have and to hold and quietly to enjoy, in consideration whereof, as also in consideration of the receiving of two thousand feet of boards, and some timber, and some labor of several persons in framing the works, I, Stephen Coffin, do consent and agree that my father, Tristram Coffin, and my mother, Dionis Coffin, shall have the use of the one-half of the aforesaid barn, coming in and going to the barn and lean-tos without any kind of hindrance, let, or molestation, by, from, or under me, Stephen Coffin, my heirs, executors, administrators, or assigns; and if my father and mother aforesaid do happen to die in some short time, as namely, within seven years after the date hereof, then I, Stephen Coffin, do engage to pay the sum of ten pounds to my father or mother's order, within one year after their decease, if they or either of them order me so to do. Witness our hands and seals to this agreement, the 18th of July, 1677.

Signed, sealed, and delivered in presence of us, who are witness to these present within written articles of agreement.
MARTHA HUSSEY. THOMAS MACY.
NATHANIEL BARNARD.

TRISTRAM COFFYN.
STEPHEN COFFIN.

This deed was acknowledged this 24th day of July, before me,
THOS. MACY, Mag.

Tristram grants his new dwelling-house to his son John.

[Nantucket Records, 2d Book, Page 19.]

To all Christian people to whom these presents shall come, Tristram Coffin, Senior, in the town of Sherborn, on the Island of Nantucket, sendeth greeting, and declareth that, in regard to my natural affection unto my son, John Coffin, now of Sherbon, as also for divers other good and lawful considerations, I, the above said Tristram Coffin, do freely give unto my son, John Coffin, and to his heirs, forever, my new dwelling-house, with all other houses adjoining unto it; and also the whole half share of land and accommodation and appurtenances thereunto belonging, namely, my part of the house lot and all commonage of timber, wood, pasturages, and all meadows, marshes, and creek grass thereunto belonging; and, I, the aforesaid Tristram Coffin, do freely and firmly by these give, grant, and confirm the above said dwelling-house, with all privileges and appurtenances as aforenamed, unto my son, John Coffin, and to his heirs: to have and to hold forever, immediately after the decease of me, the aforesaid Tristram Coffin, Senior, and my now wife, Dionis Coffin, free and discharged against all persons or person laying any claim unto the above said house or any appurtenances thereunto belonging, in, by, or under me, and in witness hereof I, Tristram Coffin, Senior, have set my hand and seal the third day of December, one thousand six hundred and seventy-eight.

TRISTRAM COFFYN, Senior.

Witness hereunto:
   JAMES COFFIN,
   STEPHEN COFFIN.

This was acknowledged by Mr Tristram Coffin to be his act and deed the 3d 10 m., 1678.

A true copy·
WILLIAM WORTH, Assistant.
WILLIAM WORTH, Recorder.

Tristram grants ten acres of land to each of his grandchildren to plant

[Nantucket Records, 2d Book, Page 17.]

All men shall know by these presents that I, Tristram Coffin, of Sherborn, on the island of Nantucket, with or in regard of my natural affection unto my grandchildren, I do freely give unto every one of them ten acres of land to plant or sow English grain on, or any other improvement, for oats, or what is fit for food for men. And I, the above said Tristram Coffin, senior, do freely and firmly give unto all and every one of my grandchildren that are now living, or that shall be born hereafter, each of them ten acres of land upon the island of Tuckernuck. To have and to hold, to plant Indian corn, or to sow or plant any other grain on, and if they or any of them shall sow their land with English hay-seed they shall have liberty to keep four sheep upon every acre during the lifetime of any one that shall so improve the above-named land or any part of it. In witness hereof, I, Tristram Coffin, have set my hand and seal 3d 10th, 1678.

Signed, sealed, and delivered in presence of us the within written deed
JAMES COFFIN, JOHN COFFIN, STEPHEN COFFIN.
} TRISTRAM COFFYN.

This deed was acknowledged by Mr. Tristram Coffin, to be his act and deed before me, WILLIAM WORTH, assistant, 3 m 10th 1678.

This is a true copy of the original by me. — WILLIAM WORTH, Regr.

By these deeds above quoted we shall learn that Trystram Coffyn had a new dwelling-house, which stood on a hill, and another dwelling-house which stood under the hill. Also, that he last lived in his new house on the hill. With this information, and by tracing the title of the new house on the hill, which was conveyed to John Coffin, and from John to his son Peter, and from Peter to his son Robert, the said Robert's estate being defined within the recollection of the present generation, I think we can know the exact spot where Tristram Coffyn last resided, and from which place his mortal put on immortality. His wife, who survived him, doubtless breathed her last in the same mansion, as she was to have a life-right carved out of the estate which subsequently became vested in John and Stephen Coffin. The Court of Sessions, at that time exercising probate jurisdiction, allowed to Mrs Dionis Coffyn the use of the entire estate of her husband during her life, the three sons, James, John, and Stephen, as administrators, so recommending."

NOTE.

P 25

Tristram Coffyn left a posterity of seven children, sixty grandchildren, and a number of great-grandchildren. His posterity is more numerous now. In 1722 there had been born 1,138 descendants, of whom 871 were then living In 1728, six years later, there had been added to the number born 444, making the total number born 1,582; and of that number 1,128 still survived. This computation, by Stephen Greenleaf, the first grandchild, was made more than one hundred and fifty years ago What the number now is will never be definitely ascertained. Their name is legion.

OBITUARY OF ADMIRAL SIR ISAAC COFFIN, BART.

["Gentleman's Magazine," 1840, vol. xiii, p 205]

July 23 At Cheltenham, aged 80, Sir Isaac Coffin, Bart. G.C.B., Admiral of the Red

This gallant old officer was the fourth and youngest son of Nathaniel Coffin, Esq., Cashier of the Customs in the port of Boston, America, by Elizabeth, daughter of Mr. Henry Barnes, merchant, of the same place.

He entered the Royal Navy in May, 1773, under the auspices of Rear-Admiral John Montagu, who confided him to the care of the late Lieut Wm. Hunter, of Greenwich Hospital, at that period commanding the brig "Gaspée" on the American station. "Of all the young men," said Lieut. Hunter, "I ever had the care of, none answered my expectations equal to Isaac Coffin. . Never did I know a young man acquire so much nautical knowledge in so short a time"

Mr. Coffin afterwards served as midshipman in the "Captain," "Kingfisher," "Fowey," and "Diligent," on the Halifax station, and from the last named was removed into the "Romney" of 50 guns, bearing the flag of his patron at Newfoundland. In the summer of 1778 he obtained a lieutenancy, and the command of the "Placentia" cutter; and the following spring he served as a volunteer on board the "Sybil" frigate, commanded by Captain Pasley, and was soon after appointed to the command of le "Pinson" armed ship, in which he had the misfortune to be wrecked on the coast of Labrador, but on a court-martial was acquitted of all blame.

Having visited England he was, in November, 1779, appointed to the "Adamant," about to be launched at Liverpool; and in the following year he escorted in her the outward-bound trade to New York. He was next appointed to the "London 98," the flag-ship of Rear-Admiral Graves, on the coast of America, and from her he removed into the "Royal Oak," a third-rate, under Vice-Admiral Arbuthnot, to whom he acted as Signal-Lieutenant in the action off Cape Henry, March 16, 1781.

In July following he was made Commander, and on his arrival at New

York joined the "Avenger" sloop. He was afterwards received as a volunteer, by Sir Samuel Hood, on board the "Barfleur 98," in which he shared in much active service. Having subsequently rejoined his sloop, he was appointed Captain of the "Shrewsbury 72," at Jamaica, and confirmed in that rank June 13, 1782. In the following December he exchanged to the "Hydra 20," in which he returned to England, and was put out of commission

After spending some time in France he was, in 1786, appointed to the "Thisbe" frigate, and ordered to take Lord Dorchester and his family to Quebec.

In the course of 1788, being irritated by some treatment experienced from the Admiralty, Captain Coffin took the extraordinary step of proceeding to Flanders, where he entered into the service of the Brabant patriots; but the event which shortly ensued, of the conduct of Lord Howe and his colleagues at the Board being declared illegal by the twelve judges, decided his return to the service of his King and country, and at the Spanish armament in 1790 he was appointed to the "Alligator" of 28 guns. At that period, when lying at the Nore, during a strong wind, a man fell overboard, and Captain Coffin, impelled by his generous spirit, immediately leaped after him. He succeeded in rescuing a fellow-being from death; but his exertions produced a severe rupture, which frequently afterwards reminded him of this act of humanity.

In the spring of 1791 our officer, having previously been to Cork, where he received the flag of Admiral Cosby, was once more ordered to America, from whence he returned with Lord Dorchester and his family in the ensuing autumn. The "Alligator" was soon after paid off at Deptford.

At the commencement of the war with the French republic Captain Coffin, who had in the interim visited Sweden, Denmark, and Russia, obtained the command of the "Melampus" frigate, in which he was employed on Channel service until the close of 1794, when one night, by exerting himself too violently, he became ruptured on both sides, which obliged him to quit his ship, and for some months he was literally a cripple On his recovery he went to Leith, being appointed to the recruiting service at that port, and in October, 1795, he proceeded to Corsica, where he served as Resident Commissioner until the evacuation of that island, Oct 15, 1796 From thence he removed to Elba, and subsequently to Lisbon, where he continued for two years, actively employed as the head of the naval establishment of that place.

Towards the latter end of 1798, when Minorca fell into the hands of the English, Commissioner Coffin was appointed to the superintendence of the arsenal at Port Mahon; and after the lapse of a few months returned to England on his way to Nova Scotia, whither he proceeded in the "Venus" frigate.

Our officer continued to perform the arduous duties of a Resident Commissioner of the Navy, first at Halifax, and subsequently at Sheerness, until April, 1804, when he was advanced to the rank of Rear-Admiral, and soon after hoisted his flag on board the "Gladiator," being appointed to superintend the harbor duty at Portsmouth. On the 19th of May, 1804, he was created a Baronet as a reward for his unremitting zeal and persevering efforts for the good of the public service.

Sir Isaac Coffin hauled down his flag on being promoted to the rank of Vice-Admiral, April 28, 1808. He became full Admiral June 4, 1814.

At the general election of 1818 he was returned to Parliament for the borough of Ilchester, for which he sat until the dissolution in 1826. In Parliament he constantly paid much attention to naval matters, and not unfrequently in a style of facetiousness that relieved the subject of its dry technicality. His charity was extensive; and within a few weeks of his death he remitted an additional and liberal donation to the Royal Naval Charity, "for fear," as he humorously expressed himself, "he should slip his wind and forget all about it."

Sir Isaac Coffin married, March, 1811, Elizabeth Browne, only child of W. Greenly, Esq., of Titley Court, Herefordshire. She died not long before her aged partner, on the 27th January, 1839, having had no issue. Previously to his marriage Sir Isaac obtained the royal permission to take the name and arms of Greenly, in addition to his own, but he relinquished that name in March, 1813.

He was possessed of considerable estates in the Magdalene islands, in the Gulf of St. Lawrence. He had crossed the Atlantic on service or pleasure no less than thirty times.

Vessels to which Coffin was attached.

Gaspée.	Royal Oak.
Captain.	Avenger.
Kingfisher.	Pocahontas.
Fowey.	Barfleur.
Diligent	Shrewsbury.
Romney frigate.	Hydra.
Placentia cutter.	Thisbe.
Sybil frigate.	Alligator.
Pinson.	Melampus.
Adamant.	Venus.
London.	

Well-known Officers in the Navy, friends of Coffin.

Sir John Montague.	Hallowell.
Sir George Montague.	Cochrane.
Graves.	Drake.
Arbuthnot.	William IV.
Hood.	Pasley.
Rodney.	Hunter.
Linsee.	

CONCLUSION.

The preface of a book usually contains its last words to the reader. Our own has long since been struck off, and it still remains to account for some lack of arrangement too glaring to escape unobserved, for which, if explained, some allowance may be made. This sketch of my subject had long been in manuscript, much more minute in detail, when invited to condense it into a discourse. In order to bring it within the specified limit of an hour for delivery, much that had been prepared was omitted. When printed for the January Record the twelve pages originally allotted were extended to nearly as many again. It was impossible, even within these limits, to embrace all that might be useful or interesting for the descendants of Tristram to know, or for the many besides who, for other reasons, should find it instructive. It seemed better that it should contain too much than too little, enough to make the rest understood.

Besides, its value depended upon finding a place upon the shelf as a volume, where it could be easily consulted, not among the pamphlets in a closet to pass out of view. It seemed, also, an object that its title should be in the catalogue of bound books in the libraries where it could easily be found. That it might not only attract attention, but be of use to the numerous class whose history it partially related, it seemed worth while to improve the occasion, without neglecting the principal subject, and incorporate whatever else would shed new light on the family annals. While passing through the press many precious documents and other papers, previously unknown, came to my knowledge; to insert some of them appeared indispensable to a full and fair view of the career of the admiral.

The writer would be glad to have copies of all correspondence that exists of Sir Isaac, letters that he wrote or which were addressed to him, and to learn all incidents and anecdotes of him or other members of the Coffin race, which if known would have added to the value or entertainment of this volume. If not his privilege to perfect this work by adding such contributions now, they will be kept together where they cannot be lost. There will be perhaps other memoirs to be written in the times to come where they will find a place. There are reasons why biographers should be of other names than their subjects. Sharing their stock and familiar with all that concerned the admiral from his earliest days, he hopes that it may not be considered presumption in him to have undertaken the task.

It has been an ancient custom, not yet passed away, for educational and eleemosynary institutions in our mother-country and other lands, to hold in remembrance the birthdays of their founders In "Pendennis," Col. Newcomb celebrated such an anniversary among the Blue Coats of London Sir Isaac, setting forth in his revoked will the rules for his nautical schools, followed simply this time-honored custom in providing that his own should be kept, and that prizes and presents should be bestowed on that day upon the pupils, that he, too, might be pleasantly remembered. He was not sanctimonious enough to be canonized for a saint, nor will it be fifty years since he died before 1889. He possessed nevertheless many of the qualifications for such a place in the calendar, in his generous consideration of others. This tribute is paid to his memory, about whom much more that is interesting might be said, on this anniversary of his birthday.

BOSTON, May 16, 1886.
19 Commonwealth avenue.

ERRATA

Page 55   For creditor *read* debtor.
"   57   For crates *read* crails.
"   67   For Brabanders *read* Brabanters.

SELECTIONS

FROM

THE CATALOGUE

OF

CUPPLES, UPHAM & CO.

ARCHÆOLOGICAL INSTITUTE.

PUBLICATIONS OF THE ARCHÆOLOGICAL INSTITUTE OF AMERICA.

First Annual Report, 1880. 8vo. pp. 26	$0 50
Second Annual Report, 1881. 8vo pp 49	0 50
Third Annual Report, 1882. 8vo pp 56	0 50
Fourth Annual Report, 1883. 8vo pp 56	0 50
Fifth Annual Report, 1884. 8vo pp 118	0 75
Sixth Annual Report, 1885. 8vo. pp 46	0 50
Bulletin of the Archeological Institute. 1 Jan, 1883 8vo pp 40. Illustrated	0 50
First Annual Report and Papers 1880. 8vo Cloth pp 163 Illustrated	2 00
American Series I 1881 1 Historical Introduction to Studies among the Sedentary Indians of New Mexico 2 Report upon the Ruins of the Pueblo of Pecos By A. F Bandelier. 8vo Boards pp 135 Illustrated 2d edition	1 00
American Series II 1884 Report of an Archæological Tour in Mexico in 1881 By A F Bandelier 8vo Cloth pp. 326 Illustrated	5 00
Classical Series I 1882 Report on the Investigations at Assos, 1881 By Joseph Thacher Clarke With an appendix containing inscriptions from Assos and Lesbos, and Papers by W C Lawton and J S Diller 8vo Boards pp 215 Illustrated	3 00

Papers of the School of Classical Studies at Athens First

Annual Report of the Committee 1881 8vo pp 13	0 25

The Second and Third Annual Reports are contained in the Fourth and Fifth Annual Reports of the Institute, respectively

Bulletin of the School of Classical Studies I Report of Prof William W Goodwin, Director of the School, 1882-83 1883 8vo. pp 33	0 50
Preliminary Report of an Archæological Journey made in Asia Minor during the Summer of 1884 By J R S Sterrett, Ph D 1885 pp 45	0 50
Papers of the American School of Classical Studies at Athens Vol 1 1882-83 8vo pp 262. Illustrated	3 00

☞ *Any of the above works sent postpaid to any part of the United States or Canada on receipt of the price*

CUPPLES, UPHAM, & CO, Publishers, Boston

AMERICANA.

ANTIQUE VIEWS OF YE TOWNE OF BOSTON
Assisted by Dr. Samuel A. Green, Ex-Mayor of Boston, Librarian of the Massachusetts Historical Society, John Ward Dean, Librarian of the New England Historic Genealogical Society, and Judge Mellin Chamberlain, of the Public Library. An extensive and exhaustive work in 378 pages. Large quarto. Illustrated with nearly 200 full-size reproductions of all known rare maps, old prints, &c. 1 vol. 4to Cloth . . $7.50

FIRST CHURCH IN BOSTON. HISTORY OF, FROM 1630 TO 1880. By ARTHUR B. ELLIS. With an introduction by George E. Ellis, D.D. Illustrated with plates. 1 vol. 8vo. Cloth. 356 pp. 6.00

SAMUEL A. GREEN, M.D., Ex-Mayor of Boston, Librarian of Massachusetts Historical Society. THE EARLY RECORDS OF GROTON, MASS., 1662-1707. Illustrated. 1 vol. 8vo. 202 pp. 2.00

——— EPITAPHS FROM THE OLD BURYING-GROUND OF GROTON, MASS. With notes and an appendix. 1 vol. 8vo. Cloth. 271 pp. . . . 3.00

——— GROTON, MASS., DURING THE INDIAN WARS. 1 vol. 8vo. 214 pp. . . 2.50

——— HISTORY OF MEDICINE IN MASSACHUSETTS. 1 vol. 8vo. Cloth 1.00

GEORGE E. ELLIS, D.D. MEMOIR OF JACOB BIGELOW, M.D., LL.D. With portrait. 1 vol. 8vo. Cloth . 2.00

RALPH WALDO EMERSON. By C. A. BARTOL. 8vo Pamphlet 0.50

JAMES T. FIELDS. A TRIBUTE. By C. A. BARTOL. 8vo Pamphlet . . 0.50

HENRY KNOX THATCHER, Admiral U. S. Navy. By ADMIRAL G. H. PREBLE. With portrait. 8vo Pamphlet 0.50

ALEXANDER HAMILTON VINTON. By PHILLIPS BROOKS. 8vo Pamphlet 0.50

DAVID PULSIFER. BATTLE OF BUNKER HILL. 16mo Cloth 0.75

Any of the above works sent postpaid to any part of the United States or Canada on receipt of the price.

CUPPLES, UPHAM, & CO., PUBLISHERS, BOSTON.

AMERICANA.

PEABODY ÆSTHETIC PAPERS Edited by ELIZABETH P
PEABODY. 1 vol. 8vo. Pamphlet. pp 248 Boston, 1849 . . $2 00
    A rare American pamphlet. It contains early papers by Emerson, Hawthorne, Parke, Godwin, Thoreau, and others

PARKER. THE BATTLE OF MOBILE BAY AND THE CAPTURE
OF FORTS POWELL, GAINES, AND MORGAN By Commodore
FOXHALL A PARKER 8vo Cloth, elegant pp 136. Portrait
and two colored charts 2 50

LONGFELLOW AND EMERSON THE MASSACHUSETTS
HISTORICAL SOCIETY'S MEMORIAL VOLUME. Containing the
addresses and eulogies by Dr OLIVER WENDELL HOLMES, CHARLES
E NORTON, Dr G E. ELLIS, and others, together with Mr EMERSON's tribute to Thomas Carlyle, and his earlier and much-sought-for
addresses on Sir Walter Scott and Robert Burns Illustrated with
two full-page portraits in albertype after Mr. Notman's photograph of
Mr. Longfellow, and Mr Hawes's celebrated photograph of Mr
Emerson, taken in 1855, so highly prized by collectors 1 vol 4to.
Boards, uncut, $1 50, or in white vellum, cloth, gilt top, uncut edges 2 50
    Limited edition printed
    "It is a marvellous piece of good printing, on exquisite paper, and illustrations superb." — *Charles Deane, LL D.*

HISTORY OF THE INDEPENDENTS Pamphlet. 1 vol
Square 8vo pp. 65 . . . 0 25
    This little book will be found to contain a large amount of information
concerning the birth and growth of the Independent movement in Massachusetts, the cause of its establishment, and its possible influence in the
future A work of the greatest personal interest to every politician, and of
the greatest general interest to every thinking man

THE EAST AND THE WEST. Delivered in Boston,
Sept. 22, 1878 By DEAN STANLEY 1 vol 8vo Pamphlet . 0 50

BOWDITCH SUFFOLK SURNAMES (Surnames of Suffolk
County, Mass) 1 vol 8vo Cloth 383 pp. 3 00

FRANCIS S. DRAKE MEMORIALS OF THE SOCIETY OF
THE CINCINNATI OF MASSACHUSETTS With plates Royal 8vo
Cloth 584 pp 15.00

DE LA GUARD. THE SIMPLE COBLER OF AGGAWAM IN
AMERICA By THEODORE DE LA GUARD 16mo Pamphlet . . 0 50
    A fac-simile reprint of the London edition of 1647

☞ *Any of the above works sent postpaid to any part of the United States or Canada on receipt of the price*

CUPPLES, UPHAM, & CO., PUBLISHERS, BOSTON

AMERICANA.

EDWARD G PORTER Rambles in Old Boston, New England By Rev. E G Porter, of Lexington, Mass, member of the Massachusetts Historical Society With numerous illustrations from original drawings by Mr G R Tolman. Dedicated to the Bostonian Society (Nearly ready) 1 vol Large quarto. Handsomely bound in cloth, bevelled $6.00

    The publishers hope to have this important work ready during the fall of 1885. Orders received before publication will be booked at the rate of $5.00

E WHITEFIELD The Homes of Our Forefathers Being a collection of the oldest and most interesting buildings in Massachusetts. From original drawings in colors. With historical memoranda 1 vol Oblong quarto Cloth, neat, gilt edges, bevelled   6 00

——————— The Homes of Our Forefathers Second part Uniform with the above, but embracing the historical homes of Rhode Island and Connecticut 4to Cloth 6.00

DANIEL T V HUNTOON The Province Laws 1 vol 8vo Paper 0 25

KING'S HANDBOOK OF BOSTON HARBOR By M. F Sweetser With 200 original illustrations Second edition 12mo, 280 pp 1 50

KING'S HANDBOOK OF BOSTON A Comprehensive, Detailed Description of Boston Classified by subjects. 350 pp. 200 illustrations 12mo Cloth, $1 00 paper covers 0 50

KING'S DICTIONARY OF BOSTON By Edwin M Bacon, editor of "Boston Daily Advertiser" An elaborate history and description of the city Cloth, gilt top, $1 00, flexible cloth $0.75, paper 0 50

PLYMOUTH, MASS Ancient Landmarks of Plymouth Massachusetts Containing historical sketch and titles of estates, and genealogical register of Plymouth families By William T Davis, former President of the Pilgrim Society 8vo Cloth, pp 312 With three maps 4 00

SWAMPSCOTT, MASS Historical Sketches of the Town By Waldo Thompson Illustrated. 12mo Cloth 241 pp. .   1 00

———

☞ *Any of the above works sent postpaid to any part of the United States or Canada on receipt of the price*

CUPPLES, UPHAM, & CO., Publishers, Boston.

AMERICANA.

OLD SOUTH CHURCH, BOSTON (Third Church.) Memorial Addresses, viz., Joshua Scottow and John Alden, by H. A. Hill, A.M.; Samuel Sewall, by G. E. Ellis, D.D., LL.D.; Samuel Adams, by F. G. Porter, A.M.; Ministers of the Old South from 1670 to 1882, by Increase N. Tarbox, D.D. With an index of names. 1 vol. 8vo. Cloth $1 00

THE SEWALL PAPERS. George E. Ellis, William H. Whitmore, Henry Warren Torrey, James Russell Lowell, *Committee of Publication.* Diary of Samuel Sewall, 1674–1729. 3 vols. Large 8vo. With elaborate index of names, places, and events. Cloth, $9 00; half calf or half morocco 18 00

    The famous diary of Chief Justice Sewall of Massachusetts, the manuscript of which is one of the treasures of the Massachusetts Historical Society. As a minute picture of the manners and customs of early colonial days, abounding in wit, humor, and wisdom, in the quaintest of English, it has hardly a prototype in the whole range of early American literature. Its publication, as an event, can be contrasted only with the deciphering of the diary of Samuel Pepys, with which it is so often compared.

    Note. — Two volumes, being the contents of Sewall's Manuscript Letter Book, are in process of annotation for publication.

EDWARD H. SAVAGE. Boston Events. A Brief Mention and the Date of more than 5,000 Events that transpired in Boston from 1630 to 1880, covering a Period of 250 Years, together with other occurrences of interest, arranged in alphabetical order. 1 vol. 8vo. Cloth. 218 pp. 1 00

CHARLES WISTER STEVENS. Revelations of a Boston Physician. 1 vol. 16mo. Cloth . . . 1 25

GEORGE R. TOLMAN. Twelve Sketches of Old Boston Buildings. 1 vol. Large folio . . 4 00

GEORGE E. ELLIS, D.D., LL.D. The Evacuation of Boston. With a Chronicle of the Siege. By George E. Ellis, LL.D., author of "The Life of Count Rumford," &c., &c. With steel engravings, full-page heliotype fac-similes, maps, &c. 1 vol. Imperial 8vo. Cloth . . 2 00

PARKER PILLSBURY. Acts of the Anti-Slavery Apostles. 1 vol. 12mo. Cloth. pp. 503 . . . . . 1 50

☞ *Any of the above works sent postpaid to any part of the United States or Canada on receipt of the price.*

CUPPLES, UPHAM, & CO., Publishers, Boston.

BIOGRAPHICAL BOOKS.

GRACE A. OLIVER. A Study of Maria Edgeworth. With notices of her father and friends. Illustrated with portraits and several wood engravings. 3d edition. 1 vol. pp. 567. Half calf, $5.00; tree calf, $7.50, cloth $2.25

————————— A Memoir of Mrs. Anna Lætitia Barbauld. With many of her letters, together with a selection from her poems and prose writings. With portrait. 2 vols. 12mo. Half calf, $7.50, cloth, bevelled, gilt top 3.00

————————— The Story of Theodore Parker. 1 vol. 12mo. Cloth 1.00

————————— Arthur Penrhyn Stanley, Dean of Westminster. His Life, Work, and Teachings. With fine etched portrait. 4th edition. 1 vol. 12mo. Half calf, $4.00; tree calf, $5.00; cloth 1.50

E. B. CALLENDER. Thaddeus Stevens (American Statesman, and Founder of the Republican Party). A Memoir. With portrait. 1 vol. 12mo. Cloth 1.00

ANNA C. WATERSTON. Adelaide Phillipps, the American Songstress. A Memoir. With portrait. 1 vol. 12mo. Cloth 1.00

MARTHA PERRY LOWE. A Memoir of Charles Lowe. With portrait. 1 vol. 12mo. Cloth. pp. 592 . . . . 1.75

JOHN LE BOSQUET. A Memorial; with Reminiscences, Historical, Political, and Characteristic, of John Farmer, an American Antiquarian. 1 vol. 16mo. Cloth . 1.00

JUDITH GAUTIER. Richard Wagner and his Poetical Work, from "Rienzi" to "Parsifal." Translated by L. S. J. With portrait. 1 vol. 12mo. Cloth 1.00

A. BRONSON ALCOTT. Ralph Waldo Emerson. His Character and Genius, in Prose and Verse. With portrait and photographic illustrations. 1 vol. Small 4to. Cloth . 3.00

CHARLES H. BRAINARD. John Howard Payne. A Biographical Sketch of the author of "Home, Sweet Home." With a narrative of the removal of his remains from Tunis to Washington. With portraits and other illustrations. 1 vol. 8vo. Cloth . . . 3.00

☞ *Any of the above works sent postpaid to any part of the United States or Canada on receipt of the price.*

CUPPLES, UPHAM, & CO., Publishers, Boston.

BOOKS OF TRAVEL.

DANIEL E BANDMANN An Actor's Tour, or, Seventy Thousand Miles with Shakespeare. With portrait after W M Hunt. 1 vol 12mo Cloth $1 50

HATTON AND HARVEY Newfoundland By Joseph Hatton and M Harvey 1 vol 8vo Illus pp 450. Cloth . 2 50

ALFRED D CHANDLER. A Bicycle Tour in England and Wales With four maps and seventeen illustrations 1 vol Square 16mo Limp cloth 2 00

J E L Ten Days in the Jungle A journey in the Far East by an American lady With vignette 1 vol 16mo Cloth . 1 00

WILLIAM HOWE DOWNES Spanish Ways and Byways, with a Glimpse at the Pyrenees Finely illustrated 1 vol. Large 8vo Cloth 1 50

S. H. M. BYERS Switzerland and the Swiss Historical and descriptive By our American Consul. With numerous illustrations 1 vol 8vo Leatherette 1.50

HENRY PARKER FELLOWS. Boating Trips on New England Rivers. Illustrated by Willis H. Beals 1 vol Square 12mo Cloth 1.25

THOMAS W SILLOWAY The Cathedral Towns of England Ireland, and Scotland A description of Cities, Cathedrals, Lakes, Mountains, Ruins and Watering Places. 1 vol 8vo Cloth 2 00

CHARLES W STEVENS Fly Fishing in Maine Lakes, or, Camp Life in the Wilderness With many illustrations New and enlarged edition Square 12mo 2 00

WILLIAM H PICKERING Walking Guide to the Mount Washington Range. With large map Sq 16mo Cloth 0 75

JOHN ALBEE The Island of Newcastle, N H Historic and picturesque With many illustrations by Abbott J Graves 1 vol. 12mo Cloth 1 00

WILLIAM H RIDEING Thackeray's London With portrait 1 vol. 16mo Cloth 1 00

Descriptive of the novelist's haunts and the scenes of his books, prefaced by a new portrait of Thackeray, etched by Edward H Garrett

☞ *Any of the above works sent postpaid to any part of the United States or Canada on receipt of the price*

CUPPLES, UPHAM, & CO, PUBLISHERS, BOSTON.

POETRY BY AMERICAN AUTHORS.

A BRONSON ALCOTT   His Sonnets and Canzonets.
Superbly printed on Whatman paper, with wide margins, gilt top,
and uncut edges. Illustrated with many photographic portraits, repro-
duced from the author's own private collection of his illustrious con-
temporaries. *Only 50 copies printed.* 8vo. White cloth, elegant.
pp 151 . . . . $15 00

GEORGE LUNT   The Complete Poetical Writings of
George Lunt. 1 vol. 16mo. Cloth 1 50

LOUISE IMOGEN GUINEY   Songs at the Start   16mo   1 00

MARY CROWNINSHIELD SPARKS   Hymns, Home,
Harvard. Illustrated. 1 vol. 12mo. Cloth 2.00

CAROLINE F ORNE   Morning Songs of American
Freedom. 1 vol. Square 16mo. Cloth 1 00

OWEN INNSLY.   Love Poems and Sonnets   With
vignette. 3d edition. 16mo. Limp cloth, gilt top, uncut edges . . 1 00

ERNEST WARBURTON SHURTLEFF   Easter
Gleams. 16mo. Parchment . . 0 35

——————————————— Poems   With
an introduction by Hezekiah Butterworth. 16mo. Cloth . 1 00

CHARLOTTE FISKE BATES   Risk, and other Poems.
Second edition. 16mo. Cloth 1 00

CHARLES HENRY ST JOHN.   Country Love and
City Life, and other Poems. 16mo. Cloth 1 25

JULIA R ANAGNOS.   Stray Chords.   With frontispiece.
1 vol. 16mo. Cloth, gilt top, uncut edges 1 25

JAMES B KENYON   Songs in all Seasons   16mo   Cloth   1 25

S H M BYERS   The Happy Isles, and other Poems.
1 vol. 16mo. Cloth 1 25

HERBERT WOLCOTT BOWEN   Verses. 1 vol. 16mo. 1 00

LUCIUS HARWOOD FOOTE   A Red-Letter Day,
and other Poems. 1 vol. Square 12mo. Cloth 1 50

☞ *Any of the above works sent postpaid to any part of the United States or Canada
on receipt of the price*

CUPPLES, UPHAM, & CO., Publishers, Boston.

POETRY BY AMERICAN AUTHORS.

EDWARD F HAYWARD Patrice: Her Love and Work. A Poem in four parts 1 vol. 12mo Cloth . . . $1 50

LEWIS The Poems of Alonzo Lewis New, revised, and enlarged edition 1 vol. 8vo Cloth pp 500 . . . . 2 00

POEMS OF THE PILGRIMS Selected by Zilpha H Spooner (A handsome 12mo bound in cloth, bevelled edges, heavy paper, gilt edges. Illustrated in photography. The poems, about thirty in number, are selected from Lowell Holmes, Bryant, Mrs Sigourney, Mrs Hemans, and other great writers) 2 00

PAINE Bird Songs of New England Imitations in verse By Harriet E Paine 2d edition 8vo. Leaflet, tied 0.50

ANGIER Poems By Annie Lanman Angier 12mo Cloth 1 50

FRANCES L MACE Legends, Lyrics, and Sonnets 2d edition, enlarged 1 vol. 16mo. Cloth 1 25

M F. BRIDGMAN. Mosses, and other Idyllic Poems 1 vol. 12mo. Cloth 1 00

——— Under the Pine, and other Lyrics 1 vol 16mo. White boards, gilt top, uncut 1 00

ALBERT LAIGHTON Poems With frontispiece 16mo Cloth 125 pp. 1 00

CHARLES SPRAGUE Poetical and Prose Writings New edition, with steel portrait and biographical sketch 12mo Cloth 207 pp 1 50

B. P SHILLABER (Mrs. Partington) Wide Swath, embracing Lines in Pleasant Places and other Rhymes, Wise and Otherwise Popular edition 12mo Cloth 305 pp 1 50

JOHN BOYLE O'REILLY. Songs, Legends, and Ballads. 4th edition 12mo Cloth 315 pp. 1 50

JAMES H WEST Holiday Idlesse New edition, enlarged 12mo Cloth. 250 pp 1 50

JOANNA E MILLS Poems 16mo Cloth 94 pp . . 1 00

☞ *Any of the above works sent postpaid to any part of the United States or Canada on receipt of the price*

CUPPLES, UPHAM, & CO., PUBLISHERS, BOSTON

PRACTICAL HANDBOOKS.

H J BARNES, M D Sewerage Systems. 12mo Paper $0 50

L. STONE Domesticated Trout How to Breed and Grow them 3d edition. 12mo 367 pp. 2 00

BAILEY The Book of Ensilage, or, The New Dispensation for Farmers. By John M Bailey. 8vo Cloth. 202 pp Portrait and illustrations 2 00

 A work of incalculable importance to the farmer, treating the new system of feeding cattle

VILLE. High Farming without Manure Six Lectures on Agriculture By George Ville Published under the direction of the Massachusetts Society for the Promotion of Agriculture 16mo pp 108 . . . . 0 25

 A wonderfully cheap edition of a famous book

THE NEW BUSINESS-MAN'S ASSISTANT AND READY RECKONER, for the use of the Merchant, Mechanic, and Farmer, consisting of Legal Forms and Instructions indispensable in Business Transactions, and a great variety of Useful Tables 1 vol 12mo 132 pp 0 50

 It would be difficult to find a more comprehensive compend of business forms and facts, for everyday use, than this valuable Assistant

THOMAS KIRWAN Electricity What it is, Where it Comes From, and How it is made to do Mechanical Work. 1 vol 12mo. Paper pp 104 Illustrated . . . 0 25

COUNT A DES CARS Pruning Forest and Ornamental Trees. From the 7th French edition Translated by Prof C S. Sargent (Harv) 2d edition 1 vol 12mo Cloth 0 75

CARROLL D WRIGHT The Relation of Political Economy to the Labor Question 16mo Cloth . . . 0 75

☞ *Any of the above works sent postpaid to any part of the United States or Canada on receipt of the price*

CUPPLES, UPHAM, & CO., Publishers, Boston.

PRACTICAL HANDBOOKS.

BUTTS Tinman's Manual, and Builder's and Mechanic's Handbook. Designed for tinmen, japanners, coppersmiths, engineers, mechanics, builders, wheelwrights, smiths, masons, &c. 6th edition. 12mo Cloth pp 120 . . . . . . $1.25

BOYCE The Art of Lettering, and Sign-Painter's Manual A complete and practical illustration of the art of sign-painting. By A. P. Boyce. 4th edition Oblong 4to 36 plain and colored plates 3.50

——— Modern Ornamenter and Interior Decorator A complete and practical illustration of the art of scroll, arabesque, and ornamental painting By A P Boyce Oblong 4to. 22 plain and colored plates. Cloth 3 50

THE GAS CONSUMER'S GUIDE Illustrated. 12mo Cloth, $1 00, paper 0 75

TOWER Modern American Bridge-Building Illustrated 1 vol 8vo. Cloth 2.00

THE MODERN HOUSE-CARPENTER'S COMPANION AND BUILDER'S GUIDE By W A Sylvester. 4th thousand 35 full-page plates 12mo Cloth . . 2 00

Being a handbook for workmen, and a manual of reference for contractors and builders, giving rules for finding the bevels for rafters for pitch, hip, and valley roofs, the construction of French and mansard roofs, several forms of trusses, stairs, splayed and circular work, &c , table of braces, sizes and weights of window-sash, and frames for the same, table of board, plank and scantling measure, &c. Also information for the convenience of builders and contractors in making estimates, making the most comprehensive work for the price yet published

DERBY Anthracite and Health By George Derby, M D (Harv) 2d edition, enlarged 12mo Cloth limp 76 pp. 0 50

POULTRY. The Raising and Management of Poultry, with a view to establishing the best breeds, the qualities of each as egg and flesh producers, their care and profit, and the great and increasing value of the Poultry interest to farmers and the country A Phonographic Report of the meeting of Breeders and Experts held in Boston, March 7, 14, 1885. 1 vol Square 4to Paper . . 0 50

☞ *Any of the above works sent postpaid to any part of the United States or Canada on receipt of the price*

CUPPLES, UPHAM, & CO., Publishers, Boston.

WORKS OF FICTION.

ANONYMOUS. Mr. and Mrs. Morton. A Novel. 9th thousand. 1 vol. 12mo. Cloth $1.25

GEORGE G. SPURR. The Land of Gold: A Tale of '49. Seven illustrations. 1 vol. 12mo. Cloth 1.50

IVAN TURGENEF. Annouchka. A Tale. 1 vol 16mo. Cloth 1.00

FREDERICH ALLISON TUPPER. Moonshine. A Story of the American Reconstruction Period. 1 vol. 16mo. Cloth . . . 1.00

MRS. H. B. GOODWIN. Christine's Fortune. A Story. 1 vol. 16mo. Cloth 1.00

———— Dr. Howell's Family. A Story of Hope and Trust. 3d edition. 1 vol. 16mo. Cloth 1.00

———— One among Many. A Story. 1 vol. 16mo. Cloth 1.00

PHILIP ORNE. Simply a Love-Story. 1 vol. 16mo. Cloth   1.25

WILLIAM WILBERFORCE NEWTON. Priest and Man; or, Abelard and Heloisa. An Historical Romance. 3d edition. 1 vol. 12mo. pp. 548. Cloth 1.50

CARROLL WINCHESTER. From Madge to Margaret. 3d edition. 1 vol. 12mo. Cloth 1.25

———— The Love of a Lifetime. A Story of New England. 1 vol. 12mo. Cloth 1.25

ANONYMOUS. Wheels and Whims: An Etching. An out-of-doors story, dedicated to American girls. With illustrations. 1 vol. 12mo. Cloth 1.25

ANONYMOUS. Silken Threads. 1 vol. 16mo. Cloth . 1.25

SALLY P. McLEAN. Cape Cod Folks. A Novel. Illustrated. 1 vol. 12mo. Cloth 1.50

———— Towhead: The Story of a Girl. 5th thousand. 1 vol. 12mo. Cloth 1.50

———— Some other Folks. A book in four stories. 1 vol. 12mo. Cloth 1.50

☞ *Any of the above works sent postpaid to any part of the United States or Canada on receipt of the price.*

CUPPLES, UPHAM, & CO., Publishers. Boston.

WORKS OF FICTION.

E. A. ROBINSON AND GEORGE A. WALL. THE DISK. A TALE OF TWO PASSIONS. 1 vol. 12mo. Cloth . . $1 00

MRS. GREENOUGH. THE STORY OF AN OLD NEW ENGLAND TOWN. (A new edition of "The Annals of Brookdale.") 1 vol. 16mo. Cloth . . . 1 00

ANONYMOUS. THE WIDOW WYSE. A Novel. 12mo. Cloth 1 00

WILLIAM H. RIDEING. A LITTLE UPSTART. A Novel. 1 vol. 16mo. Cloth 1 25

HEIDI: HER YEARS OF WANDERING AND LEARNING. HOW SHE USED WHAT SHE LEARNED. A story for children and those who love children. From the German of Johanna Spyri, by Mrs. FRANCIS BROOKS. 2 vols. in 1. 12mo. Cloth. pp 668. Elegant 1.50

    This work was the most successful book for the young issued during the season. The whole edition was exhausted before Christmas. To meet the steadily increasing demand, the publishers now offer a popular edition at a popular price, namely, $1.50, instead of $2.00.

    The *Atlantic Monthly* pronounces "Heidi" "a delightful book, charmingly told. The book is, as it should be, printed in clear type, well leaded, and is bound in excellent taste. Altogether it is one which we suspect will be looked back upon a generation hence by people who now read it in their childhood, and they will hunt for the old copy to read in it to their children."

    A leading Sunday-school paper further says: "No better book for a Sunday-school library has been published for a long time. Scholars of all ages will read it with delight. Teachers and parents will share the children's enjoyment."

BY THE AUTHOR OF "AMY HERBERT." A GLIMPSE OF THE WORLD. By Miss E. M. SEWELL. 1 vol. 16mo. Cloth. pp 537 . . . . 1 50

——————————————————— AFTER LIFE. 1 vol. Large 12mo. Cloth. pp 484 . 1 50

CUPPLES HOWE, MARINER. A TALE OF THE SEA. By GEORGE CUPPLES, author of "The Green Hand." 12mo. Cloth 1 00

☞ *Any of the above works sent postpaid to any part of the United States or Canada on receipt of the price.*

CUPPLES, UPHAM, & CO., PUBLISHERS, BOSTON.

MEDICAL WORKS.

HACKER. DIRECTIONS FOR THE ANTISEPTIC TREATMENT OF WOUNDS, as employed at Prof. Billroth's clinic. By Dr. VICTOR R. v. HACKER. Translated by F. W. TAYLOR, M.D. 8vo. Paper $0.50

WILLIAMS. THE DIAGNOSIS AND TREATMENT OF DISEASES OF THE EYE. By H. W. WILLIAMS, M.D., Professor of Ophthalmology in Harvard University. With illustrations. 1 vol. 8vo 4.00

> An important work by one of the most distinguished of living oculists. It embodies the scientific researches and the practical knowledge gained from many years' devotion to the eye and its diseases.

BROWN. THE MEDICAL REGISTER FOR NEW ENGLAND. A complete Directory and Guide. By FRANCIS H. BROWN, M.D. 1 vol. 16mo. Cloth. pp. 512 . . . 2.50

WARREN. SURGICAL OBSERVATIONS. With Cases and Operations. By J. MASON WARREN, M.D., late Surgeon to the Massachusetts General Hospital. 1 vol. 8vo . . . 3.50

> The cases cited are mainly those which came under the author's personal charge during his practice at the Massachusetts General Hospital, and the volume contains much valuable information drawn from his surgical experience.

RUDINGER. ATLAS OF THE OSSEOUS ANATOMY OF THE HUMAN EAR. By N. RUDINGER. Translated and edited, with notes and an additional plate, by CLARENCE J. BLAKE, M.D. 9 plates. 4to. Cloth extra . . . 3.50

BOSTON MEDICAL AND SURGICAL JOURNAL. Published weekly. Yearly subscription . . . 5.00

FIRST HELP IN ACCIDENTS AND SICKNESS. A Guide in the absence of before the arrival of Medical Assistance. Illustrated with numerous cuts. 12mo. Cloth. 265 pp. . . 1.50

> "A very useful book, devoid of the quackery which characterizes so many of the health manuals." — *Am. Med. Ob.*
>
> "The directions given are such as may be understood by any one." — *New York Medical Journal.*

FISHER. PLAIN TALK ABOUT INSANITY. Its Causes, Forms, Symptoms, and Treatment of Mental Diseases. With Remarks on Hospitals, Asylums, and the Medico-Legal Aspect of Insanity. By T. W. FISHER, M.D., late of the Boston Hospital for the Insane. 8vo. Cloth 1.50

Any of the above works sent postpaid to any part of the United States or Canada on receipt of the price.

CUPPLES, UPHAM, & CO., PUBLISHERS, BOSTON.

MEDICAL WORKS.

HUNT Some General Ideas concerning Medical Reform. By David Hunt, M.D., Boston. Square 12mo Cloth $0 75

JEFFRIES Diseases of the Skin. The recent advances in their Pathology and Treatment, being the Boylston Prize Essay for 1871. By B. Joy Jeffries, A.M., M.D. 8vo Cloth . . . 1 00

——————— The Animal and Vegetable Parasites of the Human Skin and Hair, and False Parasites of the Human Body. By B. Joy Jeffries, A.M., M.D. 12mo Cloth . 1 00

LUCKE Surgical Diagnosis of Tumors. By A. Lucke (Strasburg). Translated by A. T. Cabot, M.D. 16mo Pamphlet 0 25

BIGELOW Litholapaxy, or Rapid Lithotrity with Evacuation. By Henry J. Bigelow, M.D., Professor of Surgery in Harvard University, Surgeon of the Massachusetts General Hospital. 8vo Cloth. Illustrated 1 00

BOTH Small-Pox. The Predisposing Conditions and their Prevention. By Dr. Carl Both. 12mo Paper 50 pp. . 0 25

"It has more reason as well as more science than anything we have met." — *Universalist*

"Should be read not only by the physician, but by every person." — *Ecl. Med. Journal*

——————— Consumption. By Dr. Carl Both. 8vo Cloth 2 00

This is the first work ever published demonstrating the practical application and results of *cellular* physiology and pathology.

BRIGHAM Surgical Cases, with Illustrations. By Charles B. Brigham, M.D., of Harvard University, Surgeon to the French Hospital at San Francisco, Member of the California State Medical Society, Chevalier of the Legion of Honor. 1 vol. 8vo 1 00

WHITNEY — CLARKE A Compendium of the Most Important Drugs, with their Doses, according to the Metric System. By W. F. Whitney, M.D., and F. H. Clarke. 32mo 40 pp. *Specially made to fit the vest pocket* 0 25

☞ *Any of the above works sent postpaid to any part of the United States or Canada on receipt of the price.*

CUPPLES, UPHAM, & CO., PUBLISHERS, BOSTON

BOOKS FOR THE YOUNG.

CUPPLES. DRIVEN TO SEA; OR, THE ADVENTURES OF NORRIE SETON. By Mrs. GEORGE CUPPLES. Illustrated. Cloth, full gilt sides. Large 12mo. 11th thousand $1 00

———— THE DESERTED SHIP: A Story of the Atlantic. By GEORGE CUPPLES, author of "The Green Hand." Handsomely bound in cloth, gilt, extra. 12mo. Illustrated . . . 1.00

"In these two absorbing sea stories — 'The Deserted Ship' and 'Driven to Sea' — the peril and adventures of a sailor's life are graphically described, its amenities and allurements being skilfully offset by pictures of its hardships and exposures, and the virtues of endurance, fortitude, fidelity, and courage are portrayed with rough-and-ready and highly attractive effusiveness." — *Harper's Magazine.*

NEWTON. TROUBLESOME CHILDREN: THEIR UPS AND DOWNS. By WILLIAM WILBERFORCE NEWTON. With ten full-page colored illustrations, and fifteen plain engravings by Francis G. Attwood. 1 vol. Thick oblong 4to. Exquisitely colored covers . . 2.00

Being wholly without cant, affectation, or any attempt to enter into the subtleties of religious creeds, the purity, sweetness, and combined tenderness and humor, together with its high moral tone, will give it an entrance to our homes and our American firesides in a way suggestive of the welcome accorded to the "Franconia" stories and "Alice's Adventures in Wonderland."

HEIDI. HER YEARS OF WANDERING AND LEARNING. HOW SHE USED WHAT SHE LEARNED. A story for children and those who love children. From the German of Johanna Spyri, by Mrs. FRANCIS BROOKS. 2 vols. in 1. 12mo. Cloth. pp. 668. Elegant 1 50

This work was the most successful book for the young issued during the season. The whole edition was exhausted before Christmas. To meet the steadily increasing demand, the publishers now offer a popular edition at a popular price, namely, $1 50, instead of $2 00.

The *Atlantic Monthly* pronounces "Heidi" "a delightful book charmingly told. The book is, as it should be printed in clear type, well leaded, and is bound in excellent taste. Altogether it is one which we suspect will be looked back upon a generation hence by people who now read it in their childhood, and they will hunt for the old copy to read in it to their children."

A leading Sunday-school paper further says: "No better book for a Sunday-school library has been published for a long time. Scholars of all ages will read it with delight. Teachers and parents will share the children's enjoyment."

☞ *Any of the above works sent postpaid to any part of the United States or Canada on receipt of the price.*

CUPPLES, UPHAM, & CO., PUBLISHERS, BOSTON.

BOOKS FOR THE YOUNG.

SEVEN AUTUMN LEAVES FROM FAIRY LAND.
Illustrated with etchings. 1 vol. Small 4to. Cloth. pp. 136 . . $1.50

MRS. H. B. GOODWIN. CHRISTINE'S FORTUNE. 1 vol.
16mo. Cloth 1.00

———————————— DR. HOWELL'S FORTUNE. A
Story of Hope and Trust. 3d edition. 1 vol. 16mo. Cloth . . . 1.00

———————————— ONE AMONG MANY A Story.
1 vol. 16mo. Cloth 1.00

CARROLL WINCHESTER. FROM MADGE TO MARGARET.
3d edition. 1 vol. 12mo. Cloth 1.25

———————————— THE LOVE OF A LIFETIME.
An old New England Story. 1 vol. 12mo. Cloth 1.25

MARY S. FULLER. FIVE LITTLE FLOWER SONGS. For
the Dear Wee Folk. Large 4to. Pamphlet. Beautifully embossed
pages 0.50

    CONTENTS. — I. The Merry Sunflower. II. The Mayflower's Hiding-place. III The Golden-rod and Purple Aster. IV. Out in the Old-fashioned Garden. V. Ragged Robin.

BY THE AUTHOR OF "AMY HERBERT." A GLIMPSE
OF THE WORLD. By Miss E. M. Sewell. 1 vol. 16mo. Cloth.
pp. 537 . . . . 1.50

———————————— AFTER LIFE
1 vol. Large 12mo. Cloth. pp. 484 . . . . 1.50

☞ CUPPLES, UPHAM, & COMPANY keep always in stock a large line of Juvenile Books. Sunday-school and other libraries supplied at special rates. Send for catalogues and price-lists.

———

☞ *Any of the above works sent postpaid to any part of the United States or Canada on receipt of the price.*

CUPPLES, UPHAM, & CO., PUBLISHERS, BOSTON.

RELIGIOUS BOOKS.

JAMES R. NICHOLS. Whence, What, Where? A View of the Origin, Nature, and Destiny of Man. With portrait. 9th edition, revised. 1 vol. 12mo. Cloth . . . $1.00

NATHANIEL S. FOLSOM. The Four Gospels. Translated from the Greek text of Tischendorf, with the various readings of Griesbach, Lachmann, Tischendorf, Tregelles, Meyer, Alford, and others, and with Critical and Expository Notes. 3d edition. 1 vol. 12mo. Cloth. pp. 496 . . . 2.00

E. J. H. First Lessons in the Articles of our Faith, and Questions for Young Learners. By E. J. H. With Introduction by Rev. Phillips Brooks, D.D. 16mo. Boards . 0.30

"A child who studies these pages, under wise directions, can hardly help being drawn into the presence of Jesus, hearing him speak, seeing him act, and so feeling as the first disciples felt, the strong impulse to love him, to trust him, to obey him, and to give the heart and life into his care." — *Extract from Introduction.*

LOVING WORDS FOR LONELY HOURS. Oblong Leaflet, tied. 22 pp. Printed in two colors. 6th thousand . 0.50

Second Series. 22 pp. 2d thousand . . . 0.50

KNAPP. My Work and Ministry. With Six Essays. By Rev. W. H. Knapp. 3d edition. 16mo. 327 pp. . . . 1.50

NEWTON. Essays of To-Day. Religious and Theological. By Rev. Wm. W. Newton, Rector of St. Paul's Church, Boston. 12mo. Cloth. 253 pp. . . . 2.00

"LET NOT YOUR HEART BE TROUBLED." Square 12mo. Leaflet, tied. 48 pp. Printed in two colors. Illuminated covers. 4th thousand . . . 0.75

REV. D. G. HASKINS. Selections from the Scriptures. For Families and Schools. 1 vol. 12mo. 402 pp. . . . 1.50

G. P. HUNTINGTON. The Treasury of the Psalter. 12mo. Cloth . . . 1.25

BY THE AUTHOR OF "AMY HERBERT." Thoughts for the Age. New edition. 12mo. 348 pp. . . . 1.50

☞ *Any of the above works sent postpaid to any part of the United States or Canada on receipt of the price.*

CUPPLES, UPHAM, & CO., PUBLISHERS, BOSTON.

MISCELLANEOUS.

IVAN TOURGUÉNEFF. POEMS IN PROSE. With portrait. 1 vol. 12mo. Cloth, gilt top, uncut edges . . . $1 25

E. C. WINES, D.D., LL.D. THE STATE OF PRISONS AND OF CHILD-SAVING INSTITUTIONS IN THE CIVILIZED WORLD. 1 vol. 8vo. Cloth. pp. 719 . . . . 5 00

> A vast repository of facts, and the most extensive work issued in any language, on matters relating to prison discipline and penal justice.

JAMES H. STARK. ILLUSTRATED BERMUDA GUIDE. A description of everything on or about the Bermuda Islands, concerning which the visitor or resident may desire information, including its history, inhabitants, climate, agriculture, geology, government, military and naval establishments. With maps, engravings and 16 photoprints. 1 vol. 12mo. 157 pp 2.00

DIRECTIONS FOR SWEDISH SERVANTS, AND PHRASES TRANSLATED INTO SWEDISH. Revised edition. Paper . . . 0 50

SECRET EXPEDITION TO PERU, OR, THE PRACTICAL INFLUENCE OF THE SPANISH COLONIAL SYSTEM UPON THE CHARACTER AND HABITS OF THE COLONISTS. By GEORGE ULLOA. (Originally published in Boston, 1851.) 1 vol. 16mo. Cloth. 223 pp 1 00

GREENE. THE BLAZING STAR. With an Appendix treating of the Jewish Kabbala. Also, a tract on the Philosophy of Mr. Herbert Spencer, and one on New England Transcendentalism. By W. B. GREENE. 12mo. Cloth. 180 pp . . . 1 25

HALL. MASONIC PRAYERS. 4to. Large type. Limp cloth. 1 25

——— MASTER KEY TO THE TREASURES OF THE ROYAL ARCH. A Complete Guide to the Degrees of Mark Master, Past Master, M. G Master, and Royal Arch. Approved and adopted throughout the United States. By JOHN K. HALL. Morocco, tuck. 0 75

——— MASTER WORKMAN OF THE ENTERED APPRENTICE, FELLOW-CRAFT AND MASTER MASON'S DEGREES. By JOHN K. HALL, P. H. P. of St. Paul's R. A. Chapter, Boston, Mass. and P. D. Gr. H. P. of the Grand Chapter of Massachusetts. Morocco, tuck. 0 75

☞ *Any of the above works sent postpaid to any part of the United States or Canada on receipt of the price.*

CUPPLES, UPHAM, & CO., PUBLISHERS, BOSTON.

MISCELLANEOUS.

S E DAWSON. A Study, with Critical and Explanatory Notes, of Alfred Tennyson's Poem, "The Princess." 16mo. Cloth $1.00

HASKINS. Selections from the Scriptures. For Families and Schools. By Rev. D. G. Haskins. 1 vol. 24mo. 402 pp. 1.50

HOWE. Science of Language, or, Seven Hour System of Grammar. By Prof. D. P. Howe. Pamphlet. 30th thousand . . 0.50

WELLS. The Amphitheatres of Ancient Rome. By Clara L. Wells. 1 vol. 4to. Paper 2.00

HALL. Modern Spiritualism; or, The Opening Way. By Thomas B. Hall. 12mo. Cloth 0.75

RIBBON BOOKS. Compiled by Mary S. Fuller.
Loving Words for Lonely Hours. Oblong leaflet, tied. pp 22. Printed in two colors. 6th thousand 0.50

Loving Words for Lonely Hours. Second series. pp 22. 2d thousand 0.50

"Let not your Heart be Troubled." A further series. 12mo, leaflet, tied. pp 48 . . . . 0.50

By the Same Author.

Five Little Flower Songs. For the Dear Wee Folk. Large 4to, pamphlet. Beautifully embossed pages 0.50

Contents. — I. The Merry Sunflower. II. The Mayflower's Hiding-place. III. The Golden-rod and Purple Aster. IV. Out in the Old-fashioned Garden. V. Ragged Robin.

HARVEY CARPENTER. The Mother's and Kindergartner's Friend. 1 vol. 12mo. Cloth 1.25

GEORGE PELLEW. Jane Austen's Novel. A Critical Essay. 1 vol. 8vo. Limp cloth 0.50

WALTER BESANT AND HENRY JAMES. The Art of Fiction. 2d edition. 1 vol. 16mo. Cloth . . . 0.50

☞ *Any of the above works sent postpaid to any part of the United States or Canada on receipt of the price.*

CUPPLES, UPHAM, & CO., Publishers, Boston.

MISCELLANEOUS.

ARTHUR LITTLE NEW ENGLAND INTERIORS. A volume of sketches detailing the interiors of some old Colonial mansions. Thick oblong 4to. Illustrated $5.00

"To those far distant, unfamiliar with the nooks and corners of New England, this work will be a revelation."—*Boston Daily Advertiser.*

ROLLO'S JOURNEY TO CAMBRIDGE. A TALE OF THE ADVENTURES OF THE HISTORIC HOLIDAY FAMILY AT HARVARD UNDER THE NEW RÉGIME. With twenty-six illustrations, full-page frontispiece, and an illuminated cover of striking gorgeousness. By FRANCIS G. ATTWOOD. 1 vol. Imperial 8vo. Limp. London toy-book style. Third and enlarged edition . 0.75

"All will certainly relish the delicious satire in both text and illustrations."—*Boston Traveller.*

"A brilliant and witty piece of fun."—*Chicago Tribune.*

W. H. WHITMORE. ANCESTRAL TABLETS. A book of diagrams for pedigrees, so arranged that eight generations of the ancestors of any person may be recorded in a connected and simple form. 5th edition. 1 vol. 4to. Boards . . 2.00

"Cupples, Upham, & Co., Boston, we are glad to learn, are about to issue a new and improved edition of Mr. W. H. Whitmore's 'Ancestral Tablets.' No one with the least bent for genealogical research ever examined this ingeniously compact substitute for the 'family tree' without longing to own it. It provides for the recording of eight lineal generations, and is a perpetual incentive to the pursuit of one's ancestry."—*New York Nation, March 26, 1885.*

JOHN WARE, M.D. HINTS TO YOUNG MEN ON THE TRUE RELATIONS OF THE SEXES. 11th edition. 1 vol. 16mo. Limp cloth 0.50

STARDRIFTS. A BIRTHDAY BOOK. 1 vol. Small quarto. Imitation alligator, full gilt sides, $2.00; full calf . . . 5.00

An exquisitely made book, compiled by a committee of young ladies, in aid of "The Kindergarten for the Blind." Only a few copies remain for sale.

FRANCES ALEXANDER. THE STORY OF IDA. By FRANCESCA. Edited, with Preface, by JOHN RUSKIN. With frontispiece by the author. 16mo. Limp cloth, red edges . . 0.75

——————— THE STORY OF LUCIA. Translated and illustrated by FRANCESCA ALEXANDER, and edited by JOHN RUSKIN. 16mo. Cloth, red edges 0.75

☞ *Any of the above works sent postpaid to any part of the United States or Canada on receipt of the price.*

CUPPLES, UPHAM, & CO., PUBLISHERS, BOSTON.

BOOKS IN PAPER COVERS.

CAPE COD FOLKS. A Novel By SALLY P. MCLEAN
1 vol. 12mo. Illustrated $0 50

TOWHEAD THE STORY OF A GIRL By SALLY P. MCLEAN
1 vol 12mo 0 50

SOME OTHER FOLKS By SALLY P. MCLEAN A book in
four stories 1 vol 12mo 0 50

MR AND MRS MORTON. A Novel By "A New Writer."
9th thousand 1 vol 12mo 0.50

THE DISK A TALE OF TWO PASSIONS By E A ROBINSON
and G A WALL 12mo 0.50

THE NEW BUSINESS MAN'S ASSISTANT. By ISAAC
R BUTTS. 49th thousand 1 vol 12mo 0 50

THE WIDOW WYSE. A Novel 4th edition 1 vol 12mo 0 50

WHENCE, WHAT, AND WHERE A VIEW OF THE
ORIGIN, NATURE, AND DESTINY OF MAN. By JAMES R.
NICHOLS 9th edition 1 vol 12mo 0 50

THE STORY OF AN OLD NEW ENGLAND TOWN.
1 vol 12mo 0 50

ELECTRICITY WHAT IT IS, WHERE IT COMES FROM, AND
HOW IT IS MADE TO DO MECHANICAL WORK. By THOMAS
KIRWAN 12mo Illustrated. pp 102 . . . . . . 0 25

THE BITTER CRY OF OUTCAST LONDON 190th
thousand Pamphlet 8vo 0.10

AN ACTOR'S TOUR SEVENTY THOUSAND MILES WITH
SHAKESPEARE By DANIEL E. BANDMANN 1 vol. 12mo 0 75

THE ERRORS OF PROHIBITION AN ARGUMENT By
the late JOHN A ANDREW, famous as the War Governor of Massachusetts. 8vo 10th edition 0 50

EVERY MAN HIS OWN POET, OR, THE INSPIRED SINGER'S RECIPE BOOK By W H MALLOCK, author of "New Republic,' &c 11th edition. 16mo 0 25

THE HISTORY OF THE INDEPENDENTS Pamphlet 1 vol Square 8vo pp 65 . . . . 0 25

CUPPLES HOWE, MARINER: A TALE OF THE SEA
By GEORGE CUPPLES author of "The Green Hand" 12mo . . 0 50

☞ *Any of the above works sent postpaid to any part of the United States or Canada on receipt of the price*

CUPPLES, UPHAM, & CO., PUBLISHERS, BOSTON.

THE PICTURESQUE ARCHITECTURE OF NEW ENGLAND.

In One Volume. Oblong quarto Price Five Dollars.

EARLY NEW ENGLAND INTERIORS;

Sketches in Salem, Marblehead, Portsmouth, and Kittery.

By ARTHUR LITTLE.

The author of "Early New England Interiors" may well congratulate himself upon the success he has achieved in this nis first production He has chosen a difficult task on which to exercise his talents, — a task requiring no small amount of taste, and which to handle well requires high artistic abilities, strong powers of observations, immense perseverance, and a genuine inborn liking for the antique, — i e, antiquity as displayed in the now fast crumbling-away edifices reared by our comfort-loving ancestors in the old Colonial times .. That task he has done well, and in a manner that will bring upon him the obligations of that fast-growing class whose taste incline them to revering the honest, sturdy work executed a century or more ago to such the book will be a boon To those far distant unfamiliar with the nooks and corners of New England, and prone to consider the work of the Puritanical Colonist noticeable only for its lack of taste and conspicuous simply for green blinds and white painted walls, these sketches will be revelations They will ever be so to the New Englander . The credit of following in the footsteps of Nash, and of first attempting to do for New England what was done so nobly for Old England in the famous "Stately Mansions," belongs, therefore, to the delineator of the sketches before us. Many of the interiors he has portrayed, especially of those old halls where carved staircases are shown, and the ornamental work on and around windows are exceedingly well done, and the proper degree of light thrown in, here and there, to show up the architecture, and to get at a clear aspect of the whole, supposing one to be entering at the porch door is marvellously brought out, to say the least . Nothing has escaped his eye to what is interesting and picturesque — *Boston Daily Advertiser.*

A Work to be studied by all contemplating remodelling old houses.

Published by CUPPLES, UPHAM & CO.

283 WASHINGTON STREET, BOSTON